Positioning and Stance in Political Discourse

The Individual, the Party, and the Party Line

Edited by
Lawrence N. Berlin
Universidad EAFIT, Medellín, Colombia

Series in Politics

VERNON PRESS

www.vernonpress.com

In the Americas:
Vernon Press
1000 N West Street,
Suite 1200, Wilmington,
Delaware 19801
United States

In the rest of the world:
Vernon Press
C/Sancti Espiritu 17,
Malaga, 29006
Spain

Series in Politics

Library of Congress Control Number: 2020931405

ISBN: 978-1-64889-033-8

Also available: 978-1-62273-885-4 [Hardback]; 978-1-62273-954-7 [PDF, E-Book]

Table of Contents

Lawrence N. Berlin
Universidad EAFIT, Medellín, Colombia

Lawrence N. Berlin
Universidad EAFIT, Medellín, Colombia

Maria Alejandra Prieto-Mendoza
University of Illinois at Chicago, United States

Jacob Ausderan
Barry University, Miami Shores, Florida, United States

Chi-Hé Elder
University of East Anglia, Norwich, United Kingdom

Ana Maria Tramunt Ibaños, Nanashara Behle, & Yuri Penz
Pontifícia Universidade Católica do Rio Grande do Sul, Porto Alegre, Brasil

Table of Tables

Table of Figures

Introduction

Lawrence N. Berlin[1]
Universidad EAFIT, Medellín, Colombia

Positioning and Stance in Political Discourse: The Individual, the Party, and the Party Line includes original research, some of which was first presented at the 15th International Pragmatics Conference at Ulster University in Belfast, Northern Ireland in July 2017. The chapters by Berlin (this volume), Prieto-Mendoza (this volume), Ibaños, Behle, and Penz (this volume), Parini and Granato (this volume), and Martín de la Rosa, Domínguez Romero, Pérez Blanco, and Marín-Arrese (this volume), in earlier forms, were part of a panel on the same combined theme of positioning and stance. Elder, who had also presented at the conference in Belfast, was invited to contribute a chapter (Elder, this volume). Finally, the chapter by Ausderan (this volume) emerged as the result of a call for contributors organized by the publishers. The authors live and work in different countries and contexts and represent different perspectives, all of which combine to provide a broad interpretation of the topics.

The aim of this book is to present two related constructs, positioning and stance, within the framework of political discourse, primarily that of leaders. In so doing, it will be necessary not only to tease apart the two constructs, but also to relate them to the type of pragmatic work that these political actors do in presenting themselves, their respective parties, and the ideologies inherent in the platforms those parties represent.

Within the political sphere, image is crucial. A politician, like any other human being, is an individual with a lifetime of experiences and actions which combine to form the totality of his identity, both inside and outside of the political arena. The difference, however, is that, as a public figure, he renders himself open to scrutiny for the totality of those experiences and actions; and regardless of whether something occurred during his political career or before, he may be called upon to answer for it. Furthermore, a political actor is judged not only by what he does, but also by what he says and the way he says it. In many cases, verbal performance is often perceived as representative of the individual actor, standing for the outward expression of his thoughts and beliefs. Maintenance of the political public persona, then, requires active engagement on the part of the political actor. To that end, his

---

[1] Thanks to Ana Patricia Muñoz Restrepo for her help in revising the introduction.

words and deeds inform, but can also undermine his aspirations in gaining political capital (Bourdieu, 1986).

Political actors do not exist in isolation, however; they are members and, at times, potential candidates for a particular political party with its own ideology and agenda. The platform of the party, in turn, causes political actors to modify their "personal" speech to align with espoused policies of the party; if they are to gain acceptance within the party, it must become part of their discourse. But this work is not done in isolation; career politicians often have a team–coaches, speechwriters, strategists–that helps them rehearse and prepare for public presentations. And, as actors become more powerful and gain importance within the party, they may help to shape that ideology, as much as they might have previously been shaped by it. Part of the multifaceted nature of politicians, then, is that they represent themselves dually as individuals and as political actors (e.g., candidates, incumbents), as well as members and, simultaneously, representatives of a political party.

Herein, pragmatics provides a framework for analyzing the politician. As the convergence of speaking and acting (cf. Mey, 2001), pragmatics enables us to understand the intentions of the political actor by examining what he says in context. Accordingly, the aim of this book is to explore the discourse of political leaders through a pragmatic lens, enabling the unraveling of multiple layers of language use and its various contexts within the political arena. In order to accomplish this task, contributors have opted to take either a macro (top-down with the discourse as the starting point) or micro (bottom-up with the language as the starting point) approach. Beyond the approach chosen by the individual contributor or contributors, a choice has been made to foreground either positioning or stance. As this volume focuses on political leaders, the use of language in discourse for positioning or for defining stance emerges as even more accomplished than that of the average politician.

So what is the difference between positioning and stance? The contributors to this volume, as a working definition, use the notion that positioning refers to the way speakers position themselves and others–their interlocutors and their audiences–*vis-à-vis* their choice of words. Those choices are made "with respect to a context that they simultaneously respond to and construct linguistically" (Jaffe, 2009, p. 4). As such, positioning is dynamic and interactive, emerging at the volition of the speaker in response to changing circumstances or needs. By definition, then, positioning is a pragmatic act as it brings together language use in context as it is intended by the speaker and interpreted by the hearer.

Stance, by contrast, refers to the way a speaker appears in relation to an object (i.e., the physical position, mental attitude, personal belief, and/or the social morality espoused at the institutional level). It is a public act, which is recognizable, interpretable, and subject to evaluation by others (cf. Englebretson, 2007, pp. 14-15). Furthermore, stance has been conceived of as including positioning subjects (the self and others), as well as evaluating objects and aligning or disaligning with the content and, consequently, other subjects. In this volume, stance is manifest in the politician as he is represented as an individual, as a candidate, and/or as a member of a political party.

1. Positioning

The original construct of "positioning" emerged in gender studies (Feminist Theory, Queer Theory) in order to conceptualize the interface through which social and political contexts create identity as it relates to status along the lines of race, gender, class, etc. These positionings, in turn, can influence how one perceives the world and develops a corresponding worldview. Formalized as Positioning Theory by Davies and Harré (1990), and elaborated by Harré and van Langenhove (1991, 1999), positioning was conceived of in response to a more traditional way of looking at language from a linguistic perspective. Instead of a purely semantic notion of language (cf. Chilton, 2004, for a discussion of "representation"), they define positioning as "immanent" (Harris, 1980) in the sense that "language exists only as concrete occasions of language in use" (Davies & Harré, 1999, p. 32). Thus, positioning is conceived of as socially constructed rather than inherent. They have suggested that Saussure's notion of "*la langue* is an intellectualizing myth–only *la parole* is psychologically and socially real" (Davies & Harré, 1990, p. 43).

Moving into the realm of discourse, positioning is not only influenced by social and political contexts, but it constructs them and is constructed by them (cf. Alcoff, 1988). Situated within a social constructionist framework, the act of creating discourse itself is the act of positioning, "whereby selves are located in conversations as observably and subjectively coherent participants in jointly produced story lines" (Davies & Harré, 1990, p. 48). By making contributions to an interaction, then, an individual simultaneously positions himself and others through language. As such, positioning is dynamic: it is constantly evolving throughout the discourse and within the interactions by and between actors and their audiences. Moreover, through his positioning, a speaker not only presents an identity, but potentially wields influence on hearers. This is particularly relevant in politics as political actors seek to influence others through their discourse.

The act of positioning can be divided into two primary levels: self- and other positioning (Harré & van Langenhove, 1999). Self-positioning can also be referred to as first order positioning while other positioning can be divided into second or third order. Whether in the context of a speech, debate, town hall, or some other manifestation of political discourse, a politician will engage in self-positioning, often in the form of self-promotion or promotion of the party and/or its tenets. Although no pronominal[2] is required, a political actor will most often utilize some form of accompanying first-person referent, either singular or plural, as an indicator of first order positioning. On occasion, however, the politician may refer to himself in the third person, as in "A vote for John Smith is a vote for progress."

Other positioning as second order positioning is always relational and can occur directly—by having the speaker direct his speech to the person in question—or indirectly—where the speaker's self-positioning positions the other, either inadvertently or deliberately. In the former case of second order positioning (i.e., direct), the relationship exists between the speaker and the individual being spoken to; that is, the speaker positions a person or persons to whom his speech is directed (e.g., an interlocutor or an audience). Similar to first order positioning, second order positioning is often associated with a stated or inferred second person–singular or plural–referent, although the occurrence of a pronominal is not essential.

The other type of other positioning is third order positioning. Third order positioning corresponds to individuals outside the immediate interaction between the speaker and targeted hearer; that is, the speaker refers to an individual for whom the communication is not intended or who is not present at the time the discourse is taking place. Please note, however, that in some forms of political discourse–a debate, for instance–the individual being spoken about may be present, and the hearing of the utterance in such cases will indeed be intentional. Nevertheless, the presence or absence of the "other" does not alter the classification of third order positioning as the key rests in whether the speech is targeted *about* versus *to* the signified individual. Consequent to the other orders of positioning, too, third order positioning can often co-occur with a stated or inferred third person pronominal referent.

Harré and van Langenhove (1999) state that much of first order positioning performed by the average speaker is tacit rather than intentional. In other words, a speaker presents himself through verbal means that are not inherent, but arrived at through the discursive practices in which he engages. Contrastively, politicians do not typically fall into the same category conceived of by the authors; as public actors who are aware of their audience, they do much of their positioning work *intentionally*, knowing that image is a critical piece of the political persona which must be maintained at all times (cf. Appraisal Theory by Martin & White, 2003; Parini & Granato, this volume).

---

[2] While the term "pronominal" is used here, the notion is being applied widely to include the inflection of verbs for person and number.

Performative positioning of the self, or deliberate self-positioning, then, is a tool in the politician's craft, a major part of the ontological work of the political actor. Furthermore, as these actors seek to curry favor among voters in order to increase their influence (e.g., by winning votes), their manipulation of language in use is part and parcel of their performance whereby shifts in positions "involve shifts in power, access, or blocking of access, to certain features of claimed or desired identities" (Davies & Harré, 1990, p. 49).

In the chapter by Berlin (this volume), "The Positioning of Post-Truth Politics," positioning is integrated within a Critical Discourse Analysis to explore the presidential debates between Hillary Clinton and Donald Trump in their race to the White House in 2016. As one of the lenses used to unpack the concept of "post-truth" within political discourse, positioning is conceptualized as dynamic, evolving throughout the interaction. In the investigation, Berlin demonstrates how the use of first, second, and third order positioning aligns with speakers' discursive attempts to influence their presumptive audience to elect their side in this political battle.

The subsequent chapter by Prieto-Mendoza (this volume), "Positioning in the Peace Process," also uses positioning. Once again, positioning is presented as one of the tools used in a thorough exploration of the multiple layers of context and their interfaces. In particular, positioning comes into play for the analysis of the discourse (Chouliaraki & Fairclough, 1999), where the linguistic context and the interactional context merge. Looking at three separate moments during the Peace Dialogues between the Colombian government and the *Fuerzas Armadas Revolucionarias de Colombia* (FARC), the chapter presents the performance according to the proportional use of the three orders of positioning in an effort to track any changes over time. Though the verbal performance of the two sides in the negotiation for peace proceeds as expected, representative of their distinct ideologies, the shifts in their first order positioning toward an apparent alignment occur with the concurrent progress of the dialogues toward the signing of a peace agreement.

The final chapter focusing exclusively on positioning looks at the concept from a more expansive perspective. In "Oh, That's Just Crazy Talk," Ausderan (this volume) presents a survey of leaders who have been perceived as "crazy," delving into the question of discourse choices made by the leaders to evoke a specific reaction in their opponents. In moments where a dispute could result in all-out war, the positioning of the leader who positioned himself as insane, or "ready to go all the way," has led to a willingness to negotiate on the part of an opposing leader who theretofore may have been unwilling. Thus, this chapter also considers positioning as a pragmatic tactic employed consciously (i.e., the manipulation of language) to achieve certain ends.

2. Stance

Connecting positioning to stance, it has been postulated that positioning exists within stance a component that serves to establish the speaker's relationship to an object under consideration (Al-Shunnag, 2014; DuBois, 2007; Hunston, 2011). From this perspective, positioning represents the pragmalinguistic performance, which sets the stage for the understanding of the stance. In addition, this performance act of positioning, when combined with the speaker's evaluation of that object and his alignment toward or away from it, as well as other potential subjects in the communicative space, aids in the hearer's (and analyst's) interpretation. This "act of stancetaking," which falls on a scale of epistemic or attitudinal meanings, expresses a value within "presupposed systems of sociocultural value" (DuBois, 2007, p. 173). As such, the interpretation of stance is also highly dependent on context, once again underscoring the relevance of pragmatics. Until the language in use is revealed in context, meaning cannot be derived regarding the speaker's stance toward an object, the value he assigns to it, or the possible interpretation of the stakeholders and this alignment or disalignment to them.

While positioning focuses on the language use with an emphasis on the speaker's role in manipulating the input, stance focuses more on the output of an overall image, leading to the interpretation of the hearer/receiver. As seen in the first three chapters of this volume, positioning is integrated into the study of discourse as one of the tools used to yield a broader analysis. Stance, by contrast, has been studied primarily through the exploration of linguistic features to ground the analysis to the verbal performance. Among the typical linguistic features studied in the investigation of stance are modals and semi-modal verbs, adverbs of stance, and complement clauses which signify semantic categories, such as epistemic stance, attitudinal stance, and style of speaking stance (cf. Biber, 2006; Biber & Finegan, 1989).

In "Trump vs. Clinton: Implicatures as Public Stance Acts," Elder (this volume) defines stance as "the public act of positioning oneself with respect to the content of what is said, and/or with respect to one's interlocutors" (p. 73). Yet, at the risk of conflating stance and positioning, the author goes on to specify that the identification of stance markers, such as adverbials, have played an important role in identifying "the overt expression of an author's or speaker's attitudes, feelings, judgments, or commitment concerning the message" (Biber & Finegan, 1988, p. 1). Elder does, nonetheless, warn against the assumption that stance can or should be reduced to the expression of linguistic forms alone, requiring a "contextual calibration in view of [those linguistic forms] being expressed in a particular context of utterance" (p. 75). Going on to explain that stance is a public act that can also be achieved interactionally, the author demonstrates how the expression of propositional content can be expressed, negotiated, and manipulated in an attempt to achieve one's own political aims, in this case, during the 2016 US Presidential Debates between Donald Trump and Hillary Clinton.

In the following chapter by Ibaños, Behle, and Penz (this volume), stance is explored in relation to the use of expressions shared on Twitter to refer to Trump and Clinton immediately following the 2016 presidential debates. The active use of "referring expressions" (i.e., adjective or adjective-like markers used in place of proper names) in tweets as a form of expression of stance is the starting point. By offering an expression other than "Trump" or "Clinton" to refer to the candidates in the original tweet, the interactive nature of stancetaking becomes apparent as subsequent contributors respond. Thus, in the chain of communications that follow, contributors express their own stances through (a) their evaluation of the object–the characterization of the candidate given in the initial tweet's referring expression–(b) their own positioning, and (c) their alignment or disalignment with the content of the original tweet and, subsequently, the stance of the initial contributor.

Parini and Granato (this volume) in "Stance in Casting the Identity of a New Political Leader" give perhaps the most comprehensive explanation of stance. They begin by dividing the field into two perspectives, the sociolinguistic and the dialogic. Looking at the sociolinguistic perspective, the authors identify Jaffe (2009) as essentially equating stancetaking with positioning. Identifying the active and conscious construction engaged in by individual speakers, they highlight the multiple levels of contextual awareness required–target and potential audience, shared historical references–necessary to produce an effective text. The dialogic perspective, as already seen in Chapters 4 and 5, is achieved "through overt communicative means of simultaneously evaluating objects, positioning subjects (selves and others) and aligning with other subjects, with respect to any salient dimension of the sociocultural field" (DuBois, 2007, p. 163). Focusing on the former President of Argentina, Mauricio Macri, the authors integrate Appraisal Theory (Martin & White, 2005) as a framework which explores the adoption of stance. Looking at interviews conducted during the early days of his presidency, Macri can be seen attempting to construct a self-image in contrast to his predecessor and in relation to the people of Argentina.

Finally, in "Epistemic and Effective Stance in Political Discourse" by Martín de la Rosa, Domínguez Romero, Pérez Blanco, and Marín-Arrese (this volume), stance is posited along two lines: the epistemic and the effective. The former is expressed in speaker/writer statements of belief, knowledge, or evidence, while the latter emerges in expressed attitudes toward an action. Starting with the manifestos of three political parties within the United Kingdom, the authors conceptualize stance as a form of social action. They move from an exploration of "individual" political actors to the party line presented as "collective." Using a framework developed by Marín-Arrese (2011) to investigate the use of the two types of stance markers, the parties' ideologies (right, center-right, and center-left) are revealed as they adopt political positionings in their attempts to legitimize their own stances and persuade hearers/readers to support them.

The contributions contained in this volume explore various forms of political discourse and the multiple positioning and/or stances political actors present or negotiate. Utilizing clearly defined theoretical perspectives and specified social practices, the authors shed light on the ways political actors can situate themselves, their party, and/or their opponents toward their ostensive public. In so doing, the hypotheses generated and conclusions drawn demonstrate how espoused perspectives relate to or reflect on the nature of the individual political actor and his truth, the party he represents and its ideology, and/or the pandering to popular public opinion in order to curry favor.

References

Al-Shunnag, M. (2014). *Stance in political discourse: Arabic translations of American newspaper opinion articles on the "Arab Spring"* (doctoral dissertation). The University of Salford.

Alcoff, L. (1988). Cultural feminism versus post-structuralism: The identity crisis in feminist theory. *Signs, 13* (3), 405-436.

Ausderan, J. (2020). Oh, that's just crazy talk: How leaders use language to create perceptions of irrationality. In L. N. Berlin (Ed.), *Positioning and stance in political discourse: The individual, the party, and the party line,* (pp. 55-69). Wilmington, DE: Vernon Press.

Berlin, L. N. (2020). The positioning of post-truth politics: Claims and evidence in the 2016 US Presidential Campaigns. In L. N. Berlin (Ed.), *Positioning and stance in political discourse: The individual, the party, and the party line,* (pp. 1-30). Wilmington, DE: Vernon Press.

Biber, D. (2006). *University language: A corpus-based study of spoken and written registers.* Amsterdam/Philadelphia: John Benjamins.

Biber, D., & Finegan, E. (1989). Styles of stance in English: Lexical and grammatical marking of evidentiality and affect. *Text, 9* (1), 93-124.

Bourdieu, P. (1986). The forms of capital. In J. Richardson (Ed.), *Handbook of theory and research for the sociology of education* (pp. 241-258). New York: Greenwood.

Chilton, P. (2004). *Analysing political discourse: Theory and practice.* London: Routledge.

Chouliaraki, L., & Fairclough, N. (1999). *Discourse in late modernity: Rethinking critical discourse analysis.* Edinburgh: Edinburgh University Press.

Davies, B., & Harré, R. (1990). Positioning: The discursive production of selves. *Journal for the Theory of Social Behavior, 20* (1), 43–63. DOI: 10.1111/j.1468-5914.1990.tb00174.x

Davies, B., & Harré, R. (1999). Positioning and personhood. In R. Harré & L. van Langenhove (Eds.), *Positioning theory: Moral contexts of intentional action* (pp. 32-52). Oxford: Blackwell Publishers Ltd.

DuBois, J. W. (2007). The stance triangle. In R. Englebretson (Ed.), *Stancetaking in discourse: Subjectivity, evaluation, interaction* (pp. 139-182). Amsterdam/Philadelphia: John Benjamins.

Elder, C. (2020). Trump vs. Clinton: Implicatures as public stance acts. In L. N. Berlin (Ed.), *Positioning and stance in political discourse: The individual, the party, and the party line,* (pp. 71-91). Wilmington, DE: Vernon Press."

Englebretson, R. (2007). Stancetaking in discourse: An introduction. In R. Englebretson (Ed.), *Stancetaking in discourse: Subjectivity, evaluation, interaction* (pp. 1-26). Amsterdam/Philadelphia: John Benjamins.

Harré, R., & van Langenhove, L. (1991). Varieties of positioning. Journal for the Theory of Social Behavior, 21 (4): 393–407. DOI: 10.1111/j.1468-5914.1991.tb00203.x

Harré, R., & van Langenhove, L. (Eds.) (1999). *Positioning theory: Moral contexts of intentional action.* Oxford: Blackwell Publishers Ltd.

Harris, R. (1980). *The language makers.* Ithaca, NY: Cornell University Press.

Hunston, S. (2011). *Corpus approaches to evaluation: Phraseology and evaluative language.* Abingdon and New York: Routledge.

Ibaños, A. M. T., Behle, N., & Penz, Y. (2020). Discarding proper names as referring expression tweets in the Trump vs. Hillary debate. In L. N. Berlin (Ed.), *Positioning and stance in political discourse: The individual, the party, and the party line,* (pp. 93-107). Wilmington, DE: Vernon Press.

Jaffe, A. (Ed.) (2009). *Stance: Sociolinguistic perspectives.* New York: Oxford University Press.

Marín-Arrese, J. I. (2011). Effective vs. epistemic stance and subjectivity in political discourse: Legitimising strategies and mystification of responsibility. In C. Hart (Ed.), *Critical discourse studies in context and cognition* (pp. 193-223). Amsterdam/Philadelphia: John Benjamins.

Martin, J. R., & White, P. R. R. (2005). *The language of evaluation: Appraisal in English.* New York: Palgrave Macmillan.

Martín de la Rosa, V., Domínguez Romero, E., Pérez Blanco, M., & Marín-Arrese, J. I. (2020). Epistemic and effective stance in political discourse: The European refugee crisis. In L. N. Berlin (Ed.), *Positioning and stance in political discourse: The individual, the party, and the party line,* (pp. 141-156). Wilmington, DE: Vernon Press.

Mey, J. L. (2001). *Pragmatics: An Introduction.* Oxford, UK: Blackwell.

Parini, A., & Granato, L. (2020). Stance in casting the identity of a new political leader: Interviews with the President of Argentina. In L. N. Berlin (Ed.), *Positioning and stance in political discourse: The individual, the party, and the party line,* (pp. 109-139). Wilmington, DE: Vernon Press.

Prieto-Mendoza, M. A. (2020). Positioning in the peace process: Stance during the Colombian Peace Dialogues. In L. N. Berlin (Ed.), *Positioning and stance in political discourse: The individual, the party, and the party line,* (pp. 31-53). Wilmington, DE: Vernon Press.

Chapter 1

The Positioning of Post-Truth Politics: Claims and Evidence in the 2016 US Presidential Debates

Lawrence N. Berlin[1]
Universidad EAFIT, Medellín, Colombia

Abstract

The concept of "post-truth politics" has garnered a great deal of attention, especially during the period surrounding the 2016 United States Presidential Election which saw an unexpected candidate not only obtain the nomination for the Republican Party, but also go on to win the seat of President of the United States, despite the many political pundits' predictions to the contrary. What exactly is post-truth politics, then, and how did it factor into the 2016 US Presidential elections? Is it prevalent in the discourse of both Donald Trump and Hillary Clinton and, if so, to what extent? Finally, should voters anticipate that post-truth politics has become the "new norm" in politics, and are there features that enable the average voter to recognize post-truth political discourse?

Using Positioning Theory (Harré & van Langenhove, 1991, 1999), statements made by the two candidates representing the two major American political parties in the period immediately preceding the 2016 USA Presidential Election are examined as exemplars of pragmatic acts in an ostensive post-truth political era. Comparisons are made between candidates Trump and Clinton regarding their use of first, second, and third order positioning in the debates (cf. Berlin, 2015) in order to discover any patterns evinced in post-truth politics.

---

[1] Special thanks to Chi-Hé Elder and Ana Patricia Muñoz Restrepo for their invaluable feedback in the final production of this chapter.

1. Introduction

"Post-truth" as a modifier was selected by Oxford Dictionaries as its international "word of the year" for 2016 (*BBC News*, 2016). Defined according to circumstances in which appeals to emotion and personal belief outweigh the influence of objective facts, Casper Grathwohl, President of Oxford Dictionaries, claimed to have seen spikes in the use of the term in June and July of 2016. The spikes correspond, respectively, to the periods immediately following the United Kingdom's decision to leave the European Union (i.e., Brexit) in the discourse used to justify the outcome of the vote, and Donald Trump's securing of the Republican nomination for the US Presidency.

Oxford and other sources credit the coinage of the term "post-truth" to Tesich (1992) in his article about the Iran Contra scandal and the Persian Gulf War.[2] Other sources are cited for variations in its adjectival use, among them "post-truth era" (Keyes, 2004), "post-truth political environment" and "post-truth presidency" (Alterman, 2004)–the latter referring to the American presidential administration of George W. Bush during which misleading statements were made to justify the invasion of Iraq in the post-9/11 era. Essentially, post-truth politics refers to a situation where claims made by politicians are deemed or even proved to be false; meanwhile, counterclaims, asking for support, pointing out a lack of evidence, or outright denying the veracity of the original claim, are largely ignored and/or simply dismissed. Moreover, a shift in the discourse within the political domain often incorporates an appeal to emotion which resonates more with the listening audience than an appeal to logic (cf. Berlin, 2012). "Post-truth politics," in particular, is attributed to Roberts (2010, April 1, *The Grist*) in which he refers to "a political culture in which politics (public opinion and media narratives) have become almost entirely disconnected from policy (the substance of legislation)."

As an ongoing theme in pragmatics, the manipulation of language (e.g., by politicians), occurs as intentional attempts to sway the opinions of hearers (in this case, voters, toward one candidate or the other). Thus, post-truth political discourse doesn't appear so much as a series of bald-faced lies, then, but as a subtle manipulation in order to achieve a desired outcome: wielding

---

[2] The two events referred to, the Iran-Contra scandal under President Ronald Reagan and the Persian Gulf War under President George H. W. Bush, are associated with the concept of "post-truth" not through the actual events, but through the associated discourse which essentially attempted to conceal proscribed actions taken by the respective presidential administrations. Despite emerging evidence surrounding the clandestine activities, the official discourse continued to present untruths and fictitious justifications for US involvement.

influence over the hearers. For instance, in an article from *The Economist* (September 10-16, 2016), a claim made by Donald Trump, the then-Republican candidate for the US Presidency in 2016, is given as an example of post-truth political discourse: Trump advances an emotionally-charged syllogism by drawing the conclusion that former US President Barack Obama is the "founder of Islamic State," and that Hillary Clinton, his Democratic opponent for the Presidency, is the "co-founder" (of ISIS) through her association with Obama. The fallacy in his logic can be reduced to a deductive argument that Obama ordered the withdrawal of US troops from Iraq which, ostensibly, led to the vacuum that allowed ISIS to emerge, and that Clinton happened to be his acting Secretary of State at the time. Despite the obvious logical flaw and the general absurdity of the claim, the power of the utterance leads hearers to question its veracity; consequently, saying something makes it real on some level in the perception of some hearers.

Along the same lines, it is typical during a political campaign for a politician to make an appeal to the public's emotions (Berlin, 2012; 2015) since the topics that concern voters most become the focal points of comparison for choosing a candidate. Displaying opposing views to the voters on key issues could potentially sway votes from one candidate to the other, and politicians tend to organize their talking points around the differing views in their speeches. Political debates are also arranged topically around the issues. They give voters an opportunity to hear the views of opposing politicians in order to decide which one of the political choices to support.[3] A traditional view on voting has held that incumbents (e.g., sitting presidents) are considered "known quantities" and, barring an especially negative record while in office, tend to be more likely to advance to a victory than challengers. Incumbents can resort to particular achievements that are known to voters, while challengers have to make a case for themselves without necessarily possessing a widely known public record (Berlin & Prieto-Mendoza, 2014; Minow & LaMay, 2008). Clinton, having worked with Obama, who also happened to be in office at the time of the 2016 Presidential Election, could

---

[3] While the stated purpose of televised conventions and debates is to present the platforms of the political parties and their respective candidates to viewers with opportunities for direct comparison, research has shown that there is still a significant number of voters who continue to vote according to their party affiliations, regardless of the perceived or purported positions given during the broadcasts (McKinney & Warner, 2013; Warner & McKinney, 2013). Thus, the potential votes available to solicit are those of independent or undecided (i.e., unaffiliated) voters. More compelling than party affiliation, however, research reveals that the celebrity of a candidate or their likeability factor has become more influential in an advent of broadcast media as a forum for presenting options within an election (McAllister, 2016).

qualify as an ostensive incumbent. As such, her record as the Secretary of State during the first term of Obama's presidency provided fuel for both candidates. For her part, she had a record of service (in addition to her time as a US Senator from the State of New York and her time as First Lady of the United States during her husband's two-term presidency)[4] which she could use pragmatically to point to specific successful acts to bolster her position in the eyes of the voters.

At the same time, Clinton's service record could have worked to the advantage of her challenger, Donald Trump, who could also identify less successful or unsuccessful efforts as evidence which positions Clinton negatively to voters. Furthermore, Trump not only used Clinton's own record to position her negatively, but also exploited the public record of perceived negative acts or negative results during the Obama administration she served under, as well as her husband's administration when she was the sitting first lady, to position her negatively "by association" using deductive arguments. Indeed, he even attempted to extend the responsibility of perceived negative acts and results to Clinton during Obama's second term after she had resigned the office of US Secretary of State.

Trump's record, however, though outside the political domain, also provided sufficient fuel for both candidates, as it, too, was within the public domain and familiar to voters in general. His history as a business mogul and television celebrity enabled him to position himself as a "Washington outsider." Thus, although he couldn't be categorized as an "unknown quantity," he was a veritable newcomer to the political scene. His attempts to use his business record to position himself positively were met by Clinton's use of his public record to attack him as she could identify specific acts or spin others to position him negatively. Their separate attempts to highlight their own records while concurrently attempting to discredit their opponent are part of the positioning that occurs within the language games leading up to the 2016 US Presidential Election.

Against the backdrop of the candidates' individual story lines, the first question to be explored is, "What is post-truth politics?" Within the pragmatic maneuvering highlighted through their positioning during the debates, are there any identifiable features that denote the existence or appearance of what might be classified as post-truth political discourse?

The next series of questions, "How did it factor into the 2016 US Presidential elections?," "Was it a feature of both presidential candidates and, if so, to what

---

[4] William (Bill) Jefferson Clinton, Hillary Clinton's husband, served as the 42nd President of the United States from 1993-2001.

extent?," "Should voters anticipate that post-truth politics has become the "new norm"?," and "Are there signifiers that enable the average voter to recognize post-truth political discourse?" all relate to two basic classifications within the texts: moves and structures. For the sake of expediency, these terms shall be defined separately here. A move shall be taken to mean the realization of a turn or portion of a turn by a single speaker whose function completes a pragmatic act; in the case of this research, a move within the political discourse can simultaneously be seen as the completion of a positioning of the first, second, or third order. The structure shall refer to a larger exchange or interaction over several moves (cf. Sinclair & Coulthard, 1975), which can be seen to involve contributions between interlocutors in their resolution of a positioning generated by an initiator, then accepted, rejected, or otherwise modified by the co-participant. Thus, the research questions emerge as follows:

1. What feature or features signify post-truth political discourse?

2. What are the specific moves, and their concomitant functions and positionings that emerge in post-truth political exchanges?

3. What are the larger structures in which moves occur, and are there any identifiable structures which are replicated in terms of positioning?

2. Literature review

Within pragmatics, the pragmatic act (Mey, 2001) is comprised of a speech act (i.e., the speech itself and the accompanying action(s) it performs) and the context in which the speech is situated. The shift in pragmatics away from a purely linguistic approach to the study of language in use, then, is more in line with a broader understanding of how communication works (Austin, 1962; Geertz, 1983; Grice, 1975; Halliday, 1978, 1984; Hymes, 1972; Malinowski, 1923; Wittgenstein, 1958); it takes the focus away from surface linguistic features as "central" in the analysis, to afford a deeper, more situated understanding that merges the meaning of language in use within a wider definition of context (Berlin, 2007).

Political discourse, specifically the interactions between politicians (e.g., debates) and politicians and their audiences (e.g., speeches), presents a unique example of a language game. The term "language game," coined by Wittgenstein (1958), identifies the human ability to interact in order to communicate wants, needs, and ideas. Successful communication further requires that speakers have an implicit knowledge of how language works and that language possesses the capacity to accomplish things in the world (cf. Austin, 1962; Searle, 1969). Austin's initial proposal of a theory of speech acts described in *How to Do Things with Words* (1962) underscores this implicit knowledge of how language works. Sbisà (2002) goes on to suggest that speech acts are context-changing social actions; as such, they are (a) indexical of the type and nature of the interactional event and the assumed roles of the interlocutors, and (b) performative in the sense that their accomplishment can produce changes in the interaction itself, as well as in the external world. Following this logic in the current study of language manipulation in the manifestation of post-truth politics, the language used by the political actors would presumably exhibit (a) interdiscursivity (i.e., indexing other orders of discourse, such as other political speeches and debates), and (b) the pragmatic act of PERSUADING or CONVINCING (i.e., attempt to sway the opinions of voters to elect the next President of the United States).

Following the notion of context-changing social actions, then, it can be added that cultural domains–that is, the social practices and their respective discourses–also contain historicity (Bakhtin, 1981). In other words, they are produced (and reproduced) while simultaneously being recognized as (i.e., indexing) iterations of social practices through their repetition over time among specific actors engaged in particular activities (cf. Berlin, 2008; 2011c). In the case of political discourse, then, the political actors participate in recognizable orders of discourse (e.g., speeches, debates). Having historicity and knowing the effects that language can produce in a hearer afford a speaker the ability to choose their language in order to obtain certain ends (e.g., sway voter opinion in an election). Thus, a pragmatic analysis maintains a speaker-oriented focus on what one is attempting to communicate within a particular order and type of discourse (Mey, 2001).

The nature of understanding how language works and how using language to produce different outcomes within a targeted communication not only sits squarely within a pragmatic framework, but also fits within the approach of Critical Discourse Analysis (CDA). Using a CDA, Berlin (2005; 2007; 2011a; 2011b; 2015; Berlin & Prieto-Mendoza, 2014) has identified the manipulation of language in both media and political discourse as a means utilized by knowledgeable speakers to produce desired effects in hearers. While it has been argued elsewhere and in other theoretical frameworks (Lakoff, 1990; 2000) that hearers cannot be fooled indefinitely, the focus of CDA is "in the enactment or exercise of group power [engaged in by certain speakers, such as political actors, and their] control not only over content, but over the structures of text and talk [and] how powerful speakers may abuse their power in such situations" (van Dijk, 2003, p. 356).

Moreover, CDA, as an approach that examines discourse and power, recognizes that attempts to uncover hegemony in language use link recognizable social practices and their respective discourses within the notion of historicity. Consequently, through

"a specification of the configuration of practices which the discourse in focus is located within ... Such a conjuncture represents a particular path through the network of social practices which constitutes the social structure. Conjunctures can be more or less complex in terms of the number and range of practices they link together, more or less extended in time and social space" (Chouliaraki & Fairclough, 1999, p. 61).

Herein, Positioning Theory, introduced by Harré and van Langenhove (1991; 1999), is instructive in the analysis of political discourse (cf. Berlin, 2012). What makes the theory even more relevant within CDA is that the analyst can track attempts at manipulation. The positioning performed by and between the speakers evolves throughout the interaction and, hence, can be negotiated between interlocutors. An individual speaker will opt to employ self- or other positioning. In the case of the former, a speaker will present himself, directly or indirectly, to the hearer(s) and extended audience; this is referred to as first order positioning. In so doing, he may also, intentionally or unintentionally, indicate something about his interlocutor, thereby engaging in other positioning, in this case, also referred to as second order positioning. The interlocutor may accept, reject, or otherwise modify the received position by engaging in his own first order, self-positioning. The moves can go back and forth until an agreement is obtained or the particular interaction is abandoned or interrupted by another exchange. In the case of third order positioning, the form of other positioning involves the speaker referring to someone outside the communication, typically someone who is not present for the interaction. In the case of a political speech, for instance, a politician may use third order positioning to create a desired impression of an opponent–typically negative–for the sake of making himself appear to be the more qualified candidate. In the case of a debate, the "other" candidate may be present, but not a ratified participant in an exchange between a moderator and the candidate to whom a question is directed.

As a dynamic framework, the concept of positioning is not reducible to adopting a frame (Goffman, 1974; 1981) or establishing the situational context which sets the stage for the interaction (Berlin, 2007; 2011c; Prieto-Mendoza, this volume), although a frame may come along with a position (Davies & Harré, 1990). Instead, positioning emerges *through* the utterance and can progress as new positions are assigned, disputed, altered, etc. A discourse's immanent nature also recognizes that each participant enters into the interaction with potentially different understandings of roles and how they can play out, based on their cultural, historical, and social experiences; as such, political actors embody multiple roles drawn from their own personal experiences, their links to a particular political party and its ideology, and their representation of their own unique position within that party.

In addition to a general understanding of political discourse, the study of post-truth politics appears to present a unique example of how expectations, not only on the part of interlocutors, but also on the part of the hearers, can break expectations to demonstrate how accepted norms of verbal interaction (e.g., Grice's (1975) Cooperative Principle, Brown and Levinson's (1987) Politeness Theory) can be contravened. In a study of Sarah Palin's[5] rise to prominence in US politics during the 2008 US Presidential Election, Berlin (2012) specifically examines her third order positioning (i.e., positioning of others, specifically her opponents) in her political speeches to party supporters. Using a pragmatic perspective, Berlin asserts that "the speaker's words carry the power to control the direction of dialogue and, especially in the case of a politician, she can manipulate the perspectives of the electorate, if only temporarily" (p. 172). In his critical discourse analysis, he sums up one segment in particular:

> *"We believe that God has shed his grace on thee,"* part of a line from the patriotic song "America, the Beautiful," initiates a sequence of *emotional* discourse (italics added) aimed at achieving a positive effect on the audience. Its successful undertaking, however, does not diminish its general lack of relevance in actually saying anything substantive … It is an example of logorrhea *par excellence* with random quotes strung together by Abraham Lincoln (*"the last, best hope of Earth"*), Wilma Rudolph (*"potential for greatness"*), James Madison (*"more perfect union"*), and Henry David Thoreau (*government that governs least governs best"*) (… summing up with the claim that) Palin's *non sequitur* statements like *"let's not kick God out of our country"* and *"our vision for America is time-tested truths"* renders her intended meaning largely inaccessible …, save for its *emotional effect.* (p. 186, italics added)

---

[5] Sarah Palin was the Republican nominee for Vice-President in the 2008 US Presidential campaign. A virtual unknown on the national scale, she had served as governor of the state of Alaska, and was selected by Senator John McCain (Rep. AZ) as his running mate in his bid for the US Presidency against Sen. Barack Obama (Dem. IL) and his running mate, Sen. Joe Biden (Dem. DE).

Directly related to the accepted definition of post-truth politics is Berlin's (2012) conclusion that "the type of emotional discourse ... making links to other elements in the multiple levels of context (e.g., historical references that are generally familiar, appeal to current news headlines) ... constructs the effect that the lack of content could not otherwise create" (p. 187). As Aristotle explained in the *Rhetoric*, "an emotional speaker always makes his audience feel with him, even when there is nothing in his arguments" (Book III, section 7, W. Rhys Roberts, trans.). In that regard, Palin perpetuates and reifies cultural ideologies and power structures, especially when she is successfully able to position herself as "one of the people" (p. 187). And even more prophetic and evocative of the 2016 US Presidential election, he concludes by stating that

> "Her speeches, though lacking in many of the qualities one might hope for in a leader ..., *do* have appeal for an increasing number of citizens who feel far removed from Washington, DC and the traditional image of politicians; conversely, the homespun, "down to earth," "straight" talk (italics in original) represents a form of political capital that ... audience members can relate to" (pp. 187-88).

In returning to the questions posited at the beginning of the introduction, it is possible to derive the research questions suited for an investigation of the political discourse and its incorporation of post-truth politics produced by the two main party candidates in the period leading up to the 2016 US Presidential election.

3. Methodology

3.1. Texts

The texts used for the study were the transcribed versions of (a) the two televised acceptance speeches, that of the Republican and Democratic nominees for the parties' candidates for President of the United States, and (b) the three televised debates between the same two candidates (i.e., Donald Trump and Hilary Clinton).[6] The transcripts of these five texts were available

---

[6] Despite the inclusion in the race of three additional candidates for the office of the Presidency of the United States representing alternative parties (i.e., Gary Johnson of the Libertarian Party, Jill Stein of the Green Party, and Evan McMullin, who ran as an independent), the conventions were neither widely advertised nor widely broadcast—the Libertarian Convention appeared only on C-SPAN—and the candidates were not invited to participate in the national, televised debates. In fact, McMullin, having missed a nomination deadline, did not appear on the final ballot.

for downloading from online sources where both the videos of the talk and the written transcripts were available for comparison.

The respective acceptance speeches were delivered a week apart and at the end of each party's national conventions, as is customary. Donald Trump's speech from the last night of the Republican National Convention was delivered in Cleveland, Ohio, on July 21, 2016 (Peters & Woolley, 2016a, July 21). Hillary Clinton's speech from the last night of the Democratic National Convention was delivered in Philadelphia, Pennsylvania, on July 28, 2016 (Peters & Woolley, 2016b, July 28). The three debates were broadcast as follows: the first debate was on September 26, 2016, from Hofstra University in Hempstead, New York (Blake, 2016a, September 26); the second debate was on October 9, 2016 from Washington University in St. Louis, Missouri (*The New York Times*, 2016, October 10); and the third and final debate was on October 19, 2016 from the University of Nevada in Las Vegas (Blake, 2016b, October 19). The rules for the first and third debates followed the standard six, 15-minute segments with moderators presenting issues that the candidates were previously aware of; the second debate was held in the "town meeting" style with half of the questions coming from audience members and the other half coming from the moderators, but having been pre-determined through social media input from the public and organized around identified issues of concern or interest to potential voters.

3.2. Procedure

All texts were downloaded from the respective websites and formatted for uniformity of style. In the first level of coding, pronominals were highlighted across all texts using the same coding scheme; these pronominals serve as signifying tokens which can index a speaker's first, second, or third order positioning (cf. Introduction, this volume; Berlin, 2012).

Next, using fact checkers from various media sources (Farley, 2016; Gore, Kiely, Jackson, Robertson, Farley, Schipani, Gross, Wang, & Wallace, 2016; Kessler & Lee, 2016a; 2016b; Qiu, 2016a; 2016b), referenced segments from the various transcripts were identified, isolated, and coded as true, false, or "questionable" according to the findings of the fact checkers' evidence presented in relation to the claims made by the candidates. All transcripts used in the analysis were subjected to the fact checking of at least two separate sources. As a result, only those claims which were identified and segmented were used to provide the initial tokens for analysis, although the broader linguistic context was referred to in all cases where needed to yield greater comprehensibility.

All segments were entered into a table and coded initially for text type (i.e., speech or debate) and source, line number(s) in text, speaker, verity of claim according to fact-checkers (i.e., true, false, or questionable), positioning (first, second, or third order), and pronominal use (first, second, or third person, singular or plural) in order to allow for easier analysis and the possible identification of patterning. In the final analysis and in line with the focus of this research–identifying iterations of post-truth claims and their underlying structures for classification–only those claims that were identified by fact-checkers as false were included.

The segmentation of the transcripts yielded a total of 191 tokens which had been checked for factualness (see Table 1.1). In a few cases, repetitions were counted as individual tokens where they were separated by another individual's turn at talk and where they represented a subsequent move by the same speaker. Of the total number of segments identified, 128/191 or 67% of those were stated claims made by Mr. Trump, and 63/191 or 33% were stated claims made by Mrs. Clinton. Looking at the two candidates' contributions separately, Trump's claims were determined to be as follows according to fact-checkers: 20% True; 18% Questionable; and 62% False. Contrastively, Clinton's claims were determined to be as follows: 63% True; 27% Questionable; and 10% False.

Table 1.1. Claims submitted for fact-checking in
2016 US Presidential Election Campaign

		True			Quest			False			
		Claim	%SELF	%TOT	Claim	%SELF	%TOT	Claim	%SELF	%TOT	TOT *N*
DT	A1	7			6			12			25
	D1	7			8			21			36
	D2	10			5			27			42
	D3	1			4			20			25
		25	20%	13%	23	18%	12%	80	62%	42%	128
HC	A2	6			6			0			12
	D1	19			3			0			22
	D2	9			3			4			16
	D3	6			5			2			13
		40	63%	21%	17	27%	9%	6	10%	3%	63
		65		34%	40		21%	86		45%	191

From the 191 tokens obtained, a total of 86 claims were identified as false by fact-checkers, representing 45% of the total number of original segments; of these, 80 or 93% of the total number of false claims (n=86) were made by Trump, and 6 or 7% of the total number of false claims were made by Clinton. These 86 segments became the data tokens which were analyzed for the current study investigating post-truth claims and their positioning occurring in political discourse, specifically within the context of the final weeks leading up to the 2016 US Presidential Election, after the candidates for the two major parties within the United States had been identified and from the time they accepted their respective party's nominations.

3.3. Analysis

The original transcripts from the 2016 US Presidential Campaign comprised both acceptance speeches made by the candidates from the two main political parties in the United States, as well as three separate debates in which the two candidates participated. An initial examination of the transcripts and the portions that had been identified as claims having been subjected to fact checking by professional political pundits led to the extraction of 86 segments for analysis. These 86 segments were identified by at least two different fact checking sources as false in content, thus rendering them the data to be analyzed in attempting to answer the central research question relating to the nature and structure of post-truth claims in political discourse.

As detailed in the previous section, each segment had been coded for text type (i.e., acceptance speech or debate) and source, line number(s) in text, speaker, positioning (first, second, or third order), and pronominal use (first, second, or third person, singular or plural). In response to the first research question regarding the nature of features in post-truth claims which could signify the use of emotion over logic in appealing to potential voters (Berlin, 2012; 2015), segments were explored for linguistic components (i.e., signifiers) which could denote post-truth as readily identifiable.

In attempting to respond to the second research question, all segments were broken down according to their use of first, second, or third order positioning and their pragmatic function by generating categories which signified the underlying purpose of the move. These were, in turn, situated within the larger structure to determine whether patterning showed any consistencies within and across texts; these were then used to generate a classification table which emerged from the data in order to render the findings more accessible (See Table 1.2, next section).

3.4. Findings and Discussion

Table 1.2. Structure of post-truth claims and interactions

Move I	CLM (Claim without Emotional Appeal) Δ	(Self Dir.) 1st Order Positioning
	CLE (Claim with Emotional Appeal) Δ	(Other Dir.) 2nd Order Positioning w/moderator 3rd Order Positioning w/opponent
Move II	DEN (Denial) "No, I don't/didn't/wasn't." †	1st Order Positioning
	RDR (Redirect/Change of Topic) "I'd like to talk about…" ‡ Δ	
	DIS (Dismissal) "You don't know what you're talking about." † ‡	2nd Order Positioning
	CAT (Counterattack) "She/He {negative} + CLM/CLE" † ‡ Δ	(2nd or) 3rd Order Positioning
	CCL (Counterclaim) "The evidence shows…" † ‡ Δ	
Move III	(I) RCL ((Repetition of Original Claim/Assertion) † Δ	1st, 2nd, or 3rd (See Move I: CLM / CLE)
	DEN (Denial) "No, I don't/didn't/wasn't." †	1st Order Positioning
	RDR (Redirect/Change of Topic) "I'd like to talk about…" ‡ Δ	
	DIS (Dismissal) "You don't know what you're talking about." † ‡	2nd Order Positioning
	CAT (Counterattack) "She/He {negative} + CLM/CLE" † ‡ Δ	(2nd or) 3rd Order Positioning
	CCL (Counterclaim) "The evidence shows…" † ‡ Δ	

Key: † Challenge ‡ Evasion Δ Syllogism (Note: A request for support or evidence can also serve as a challenge †)

The initial move (cf. Sinclair & Coulthard, 1975) for the analytic framework used in this discourse analysis is always the initial claim or assertion made by a speaker. Claims originating from the texts examined in this research are found to include examples both without an emotional appeal (CLM) or with an emotional appeal (CLE), as can be seen in (1) and (2).[7]

(1)

D1. TRUMP: 617 [CLM. But you will learn more about Donald Trump by going down to the federal

618 elections, where I filed a 104-page essentially financial statement of sorts, the forms

619 that they have.] It shows income–in fact, the income–I just looked today–the income

620 is filed at $694 million for this past year, $694 million. If you would have told me I was

621 going to make that 15 or 20 years ago, I would have been very surprised.

In (1), Trump is making a claim about what he has done to be transparent about his income—an issue which comes up in nearly every election about the candidates' filing of tax returns to demonstrate their good faith in taking care of a civic responsibility. Since Trump had not made his tax returns available to the public, it became a question about his transparency and sense of duty as a citizen. His assertion in (1) is not considered an emotional appeal as he does not use any devices to embellish his claim, but rather states plainly what he wants the listening audience to know about his income.

(2)

A1. TRUMP: 405 most important issues decided by this election. [CLE. My opponent

406 wants to essentially abolish the 2nd amendment.] I, on the other hand,

407 received the early and strong endorsement of the National Rifle

---

[7] In the excerpts provided for example, the following notations can be understood as follows: Segments are initially marked for source. "A" refers to acceptance speech, 1 being Trump's which occurred first; "D" refers to debate and the subsequent numbers indicate which of the three the segment came from. Brackets "[" and "]" demarcate the start and end of a claim; underlining "___" indicates the false claim, as identified through at least two sources of fact-checking; double underlining "___" is used for the purpose of highlighting a portion of the text which will be referenced in the discussion that follows the segment.

> 408 Association and will protect the right of all
> Americans to keep their
>
> 409 families safe.

In (2), Trump precedes his claim with the phrase "most important issues" before positioning Clinton as wanting to "abolish the 2nd amendment."[8] Thus, by the mention of an especially controversial issue, he positions Clinton as someone who is planning to "abolish" an amendment which is part of the Bill of Rights, among the most sacrosanct components of the US Constitution for American people. This negative assessment is juxtaposed with his own positioning of himself in the subsequent lines as a protector of the Constitution and the choice that will protect rights and "keep ... families safe." His references resonate with many listeners as the belief that possessing guns as a means to securing one's home and the "endorsement of the National Rifle Association"[9] adhere to a certain belief system that remains entrenched in the mindset of a large number of Americans.

Another example can be seen in (3), where Trump prefaces his CLE by announcing that he will say something "very important" before mentioning ISIS,[10] another heated issue, and then suggesting that Clinton was jointly responsible for its formation (lines 1371-1373). Using the term "disaster" twice, in line 1373 and shortly thereafter in 1384 where he boosts the reference to be just one among many of "her disasters," Trump addresses the audience with third order positioning where Clinton is seen to be at fault for ISIS' very existence ("And ISIS was formed.").

---

[8] The Second Amendment to the Constitution of the United States is generally known as the "Right to Bear Arms" and, either due to the perceived sanctity of the Bill of Rights in the Constitution or the love of guns, the issues surrounding gun ownership in the United States and the mere mention of restricting rights of gun owners always provokes a polemic discussion.

[9] The National Rifle Association (NRA) is not merely a club that boasts a wide membership among gun owners in the United States, but it has become a major political force as its lobby for or against candidates wields a great deal of influence in Washington and among voters nationwide.

[10] ISIS, or the Islamic State of Iraq and Syria, also known as ISIL or Da'esh, is believed to have emerged from an offshoot of Al-Qaeda after the US invasion of Iraq. Primarily formed among Sunni Muslims who rejected the invasion and ongoing presence of foreigners in their land, as well as the subsequent formation of a multiethnic ruling government in Iraq, its aim was to establish a worldwide caliphate under strict sharia law. Its largest seizure of territory covered much of Iraq and Syria, and its repression of local populations included the forced conversion or slaughter of thousands. ISIS has been labeled a terrorist group by the United Nations and its adherents continue to attempt to recruit and annex land for its cause in different parts of the world.

(3)

D1. TRUMP: 1369 Well, first I have to say one thing, <u>very important</u>.
Secretary Clinton is talking

1370 about taking out ISIS. "We will take out ISIS." Well,
[CLE. <u>President Obama and</u>

1371 Secretary Clinton created a vacuum the way they
got out of Iraq, because they got out

1372 what, they shouldn't have been in, but once they
got in, the way they got out was a

1373 <u>disaster</u>. And ISIS was formed.]

1374 ...

1381 ... [CLE. had we taken the oil–and we should have
taken the oil–ISIS would not

1382 have been able to form either, because the oil was
their primary source of income. And

1383 now they have the oil all over the place, including
the oil–a lot of the oil in Libya,

1384 which was another one of <u>her disasters</u>.]

In this excerpt, a specific device that Trump uses throughout the campaign can be found. Efforts to discredit opponents, especially in the case of a challenger candidate trying to unseat an incumbent, may be supported through the use of association, connecting the incumbent not necessarily to his or her own acts, but to the acts of an associate. Herein can be found the use of a syllogistic fallacy in post-truth politics, specifically the "fallacy of necessity" whereby the unwarranted focus tends to be on the conclusion rather than the internal logic leading to a logical conclusion. Trump's compound use in the first part (lines 1370 and 1371) of "President Obama and Secretary Clinton" sets the pragmatic stage for what comes next. He need not state that he considers them directly responsible; he simply needs to juxtapose two pieces of information in the manner of a deductive argument where the interpretation appears to lead to a "logical" conclusion: "the way they got out was a disaster. And ISIS was formed." The second part of the excerpt presents a further example of this type of guilt by association where he shifts from Iraq to Libya and asserts that (line 1383) "they (ISIS) have the oil all over the place, including ... in Libya" and that represents "another one of [Clinton's] disasters."[11]

One of the features that often emerges within the data in this research is the alignment between a CLM and a CLE with the type of positioning. The CLM tends to occur with first order positioning or self-positioning. The CLE, in contrast, tends to occur with other positioning, most frequently a form of second order positioning in interactions with the moderators in debates, and a form of third order positioning in interactions with political opponents; that is, when the speaker is reacting to something an opponent has said, he or she will direct the talk to the audience and make an emotional claim about the rival. As seen in (2) and (3), this may also be accompanied with self-positioning statements, but the CLE itself is a clear example of audience-directed, third order positioning of Clinton. In terms of an exchange, however, both CLMs and CLEs can be used in the analysis to demarcate the first or initial move in an interaction (I).

Advancing to the second move or response (R) to the initial move in an interaction, five strategies are found within the data. These are labeled according to their patterns and positionings; they are, in turn, the denial (DEN), the redirect or change of topic (RDR), the dismissal (DIS), the counterattack (CAT), and the counterclaim (CCL). Each is discussed in terms of its positioning and pattern.

The first two strategies, DEN and RDR, exhibit a speaker's first order positioning; in the first case, the DEN proceeds from where the individual has just been the recipient of other positioning—second or third order—and is challenging that position by using self-positioning combined with a negative modifier, reinforcing the rejection of the received claim, as seen in (4) and (5):

(4)

D1. CLINTON: 1388 CCL. Well, I hope the fact-checkers are turning up the volume and really

1389 working hard. Donald supported the invasion of Iraq.

1390

TRUMP: 1391 [DEN. Wrong.]

---

[11] The reference to Libya juxtaposed with Clinton also raises the specter of another event during Clinton's term as Secretary of State during the first Obama administration which can be damaging to her: the attack on the US Consulate in Benghazi and the assassination of several key staff members, including the then US Ambassador to Libya, J. Christopher Stevens, in September 2012.

	1392
CLINTON:	1393 RCL. That is absolutely proved over and over again.
	1394
TRUMP:	1395 [DEN. Wrong. Wrong.]
	1396
CLINTON:	1397 CCL. He actually advocated for the actions we took in Libya and urged that
	1398 Gadhafi be taken out, after actually doing some business with him one time.

(5)

D1. CLINTON: 1810 You know, he tried to switch from looks to stamina. CLE. But this is a man

1811 who has called women pigs, slobs and dogs, and someone who has said pregnancy is an

1812 inconvenience to employers, who has said...

1813

TRUMP: 1814 [DEN. I never said that.]

1815

CLINTON: 1816 CLE.....women don't deserve equal pay unless they do as good a job as men.

1817

TRUMP: 1818 [DEN. I didn't say that.]

1819

CLINTON: 1820 CLE. And one of the worst things he said was about a woman in a beauty

1821 contest. He loves beauty contests, supporting them and hanging around them. And he

1822 called this woman "Miss Piggy." Then he called her "Miss Housekeeping," because she

1823 was Latina. Donald, she has a name.

1824

TRUMP: 1825 RFE. Where did you find this? Where did you find this?

1826

CLINTON: 1827 Her name is Alicia Machado.

1828

TRUMP: 1829 RFE. Where did you find this?

The DEN is thus a challenge to other positioning, using a rejection of the interlocutor's attempt, as in (4), lines 1391 and 1395, where Trump states that the assertion is "Wrong" (by extension "[You are/She is] wrong"), while still possessing the first order positioning in the subtext, "No, I didn't." Support for the analyst's interpretation regarding subtext comes forth in excerpt (5), lines 1814 and 1818 when Trump responds respectively with "I never said that" and "I didn't say that," despite the fact that both quotes attributed to him by Clinton are part of the public record.

Both (4) and (5) present examples of a unique feature from the data where the interaction (or apparent lack of interaction) proceeds as a sort of initiative-response (cf. Sinclair & Coulthard, 1975) chain in the discourse (i.e., I, R, I, R, …) where the third move occurs more as a continuation or repetition of the first move, rather than an attempt to resolve the communication. The nature of this occurrence could be due to the fact that the actual interlocutor for the speaker of the first move is the audience, not her or his opponent. Consequently, the move following the challenge ostensibly ignores the interruption of the second move.

An interesting follow-up feature which appears only a few times in the data is the request for evidence (RFE). This can be seen in (5), lines 1825 and 1829, where Trump repeatedly insists that Clinton provide evidence for her claims, asking "Where did you find this?" Perhaps he believes that this form of challenge will be sufficient to dismiss the verity of Clinton's assertions. The strategy, however, is not included in Table 1.2 as it does not conform to the requisite fact-checking test of the other strategies identified, although further research may prove it to be a unique feature of post-truth political discourse.

Another type of second move (R) which also takes on the form of first order or self-positioning is the redirect (RDR). In this strategy, the opponent attempts to change the direction of talk or the topic itself. Inasmuch as the strategy breaks the expectations of adherence to cooperative communication, it is a feature that is typical in political discourse whereby the politician, when given the opportunity to respond to a claim, coopts the direction of talk for his or her own benefit. An example of this can be found in (6) where Trump takes several turns to actually answer the claim made by Anderson Cooper (a moderator in the second debate) in lines 99 through 101, before shifting into a redirect in lines 112-115.

(6)

D2. COOPER: 99 CLE. Just for the record, though, are you saying that what you said on that bus 11

100 years ago that you did not actually kiss women without consent or grope women

101 without consent?

...

TRUMP: 107 I've said things that, frankly, you hear these things I said. And I was

108 embarrassed by it. But I have tremendous respect for women.

109

COOPER: 110 Have you ever done those things?

111

TRUMP: 112 And women have respect for me. And I will tell you: No, I have not. [RDR. And I

113 will tell you that I'm going to make our country safe. We're going to have borders in our

114 country, which we don't have now. People are *pouring* into our country, and they're

115 coming in from the *Middle East* and other places.]

Thus, while the audience has the impression that Trump is about to confess to abusive behavior toward women in lines 107 and 108 ("I've said things that, frankly, you hear these things I said. And I was embarrassed by it."), he counters with a denial in line 112 ("No, I have not."). The denial is immediately followed by the use of a redirect which breaks the logical thread of the talk by introducing an unrelated issue (i.e., illegal immigration and keeping the borders safe), boosted by the assertion that "People are *pouring* into our country" and focusing attention on the "Middle East" as their point of origin. This thread is meant to heighten the emotional involvement of the audience as they will undoubtedly (in Trump's mind) make a connection to other concepts that he often repeats and relates to one another, such as "radical Islam" and "terrorism" in the basest form of fomenting fear.

The next strategy employed in the second move (R) is other directed, but specifically aimed at the interlocutor. In the dismissal (DIS), the response of the politician targeted by the initial speaker takes the form of second order positioning where the competence, as well as the veracity, of the first speaker in the interaction is brought into question by a challenge which essentially equates to "You don't know what you're talking about," as can be seen in (7).

(7)

D3. TRUMP: 904 [DIS.The problem is, you talk, but you don't get anything done, Hillary. You don't.] [CAT.

905 Just like when you ran the State Department, $6 billion was missing. How do you miss

906 $6 billion? You ran the State Department, $6 billion was either stolen. They don't know.

907 It's gone, $6 billion. If you become president, this country is going to be in some mess.

908 Believe me.]

Trump is given the floor following Clinton's claim that he has outsourced goods and services for his own companies in spite of his campaign promises to put American companies first. He retorts that Clinton had the chance to put American companies first for all the years she held office. He then dismisses her claim, as well as her ability to accomplish anything effectively while in office by directly stating in line 904, "The problem is, you talk, but you don't get anything done, Hillary."

In (7), another strategy, the counterattack (CAT) also emerges as part of the second move. The distinguishing feature between the DIS and the CAT is the inclusion of a new claim in the CAT. Beginning in line 905, Trump's dismissal of Clinton's effectiveness in office offers an example where he counters her claim regarding his inexperience with his own claim in line 905 about missing funds during her term as US Secretary of State: "Just like when you ran the State Department, $6 billion was missing."

Counterattacks, while being other-directed, can appear with both second order positioning, as in (7), or third order positioning, as in (8):

(8)

D2. COOPER: 1424 The question is, is that the discipline of a good leader?

1425

TRUMP: 1426 ... 600–wait a minute, Anderson, 600 times. Well, she said she was awake at 3

1427 o'clock in the morning, and she also sent a tweet out at 3 o'clock in the morning, but I

1428 won't even mention that. But she said she'll be awake. Who's going–the famous thing,

1429 we're going to answer our call at 3 o'clock in the morning. Guess what happened?

[CAT.

1430 Ambassador Stevens–Ambassador Stevens sent 600 requests for help. And the only

1431 one she talked to was Sidney Blumenthal, who's her friend and not a good guy, by the

1432 way. So, you know, she shouldn't be talking about that.]

Responding to Cooper's restating of his original question regarding the use of Twitter at 3 o'clock in the morning to defame others, particularly referencing a sex tape made by one of his detractors, Trump argues that Clinton also used Twitter at the same hour. His CAT, however, maintains the use of third order positioning throughout while referring to Clinton, who is present, but not part of the immediate interaction. He returns to a reference of "Ambassador Stevens" made earlier during the same debate (cf. footnote 10), focusing on Clinton's inappropriateness by alleging that she didn't respond to "600 requests for help" (line 1430), but rather "talked to ... Sidney Blumenthal" (line 1431) about the matter which he represents as a break in protocol: "So, you know, she shouldn't be talking about that." (line 1432).

The final strategy that emerges in the second move within the transcripts is the counterclaim (CCL). The CCL follows the other-directed nature of positioning, but exclusively uses third order positioning. Excerpt (9) provides an extended example in the interaction:

(9)

D2.CLINTON: 820 CLE. We have never in the history of our country been in a situation where an

821 adversary, a foreign power, is working so hard to influence the outcome of the election.

822 And believe me, they're not doing it to get me elected. They're doing it to try to influence

823 the election for Donald Trump.

824

825 Now, maybe because he has praised Putin, maybe because he says he agrees

826 with a lot of what Putin wants to do, maybe because he wants to do business in Moscow,

827 I don't know the reasons. But we deserve answers. And we should demand that Donald

828 release all of his tax returns so that people can see what are the entanglements and the

829 financial relationships that he has…

…

CLINTON: 833 … with the Russians and other foreign powers.

…

TRUMP: 848 But as far as other elements of what she was saying, [DEN. I don't know Putin.] I think it

849 would be great if we got along with Russia because we could fight ISIS together, as an

850 example. [DEN. But I don't know Putin.]

851

852 [CCL. But I notice, anytime anything wrong happens, they like to say the Russians are–

853 she doesn't know if it's the Russians doing the hacking. Maybe there is no hacking. But

854 they always blame Russia. And the reason they blame Russia because they think they're

855 trying to tarnish me with Russia.] [DEN. I know nothing about Russia. I know–I know

856 about Russia, but I know nothing about the inner workings of Russia. I don't deal there. I

857 have no businesses there. I have no loans from Russia.]

The counterclaim (CCL) differs from the CAT through a shift away from a direct focus on the opponent to the evidence being offered. In (9), Trump uses his second move (R) to challenge Clinton's allegations regarding his possible involvement with the Russians. Immediately following two denials in lines 848 and 850, he focuses on the ongoing attempts by the Clinton campaign to link him to Russia, starting in line 852: "But I notice, anytime anything wrong happens, they like to say the Russians are … they always blame Russia. … they're trying to tarnish me with Russia." This iteration of the CCL is followed by even more denials before Trump concludes his turn.

Returning to Table 1.2, it is apparent that the strategies found in the second move of interactions are identical to the strategies employed in the third move, or follow-up (F), when it occurs. As previously mentioned, two patterns of interactions were found: those that seemed to follow a relatively normal sequence with the resolution of an exchange in two or three moves (I-R, I-R-F)–although the moves by a single participant could be rather extended and would likely include a combination of strategies–and those that followed a chain sequence whereby the interaction didn't seem to be resolved, but continued in a veritable repetition of the initiative-response with no immediate resolution coming in a third or subsequent turn until the chain was interrupted by a moderator or finally managed to get resolved of its own accord (cf. excerpts 4 and 5). In some cases, especially where there seems to be some kind of break in the interaction sequence, a final strategy that was identified in the data has been categorized as the repetition of the original claim/assertion (RCL). While another analyst might classify the occurrence of this strategy as simply another CLM or CLE in a chain sequence, one distinguishing feature is the anaphoric nature which seems to be a key to the RCL, as in (10):

(10)

D3. TRUMP: 706 Well, first of all, before I start on my plan, her plan is going to raise taxes and

707 even double your taxes. Her tax plan is a disaster. And she can say all she wants about

708 college tuition. And I'm a big proponent. We're going to do a lot of things for college

709 tuition. But the rest of the public's going to be paying for it. We will have a massive,

710 massive tax increase under Hillary Clinton's plan.

711

712 But I'd like to start off where we left, because when I said Japan and Germany,

713 and I'm – not to single them out, but South Korea, these are very rich, powerful

714 countries. Saudi Arabia, nothing but money. We protect Saudi Arabia. Why aren't they

715 paying?

716

717 [RCL. She immediately – when she heard this, I
questioned it, and I questioned NATO.

718 Why aren't the NATO questioned – why aren't they
paying? Because they weren't

719 paying. Since I did this – this was a year ago – all of a
sudden, they're paying. And I've

720 been given a lot – a lot of credit for it. All of a sudden,
they're starting to pay up. They

721 have to pay up. We're protecting people, they have to
pay up. And I'm a big fan of NATO.

722 But they have to pay up.]

The sequence proceeds accordingly: Clinton offers her plan to create jobs
under her leadership (I). Mike Wallace, the moderator for the third debate,
prompts Trump to present his plan (R). In his follow-up (F), the third move in
the sequence, Trump begins with his assessment of Clinton's plan in line 706,
ultimately evaluating the plan as "a disaster" (line 707) and claiming that it
would create "a massive, massive tax increase" (lines 709-710). He then goes
on to clarify an issue that had been raised earlier in the debate in line 712. In
line 717, he generates the RCL by citing Clinton's reference to his comments
on NATO and the need for other member states to "pay up" (line 720). He
erroneously takes credit for the power of his earlier words as bringing about a
change in protocol: "Since I did this ..., they're paying." (line 719). Thus, his
post-truth political assertion which returns to an earlier point made during
the same discourse (i.e., Debate 3) occurs here as a follow-up to an
interlocutor response and his third move (F) can be labeled as a repetition of a
previous claim (RCL), as opposed to an initial CLM or CLE.

4. Conclusions

Returning to the research questions for the study, we find that the answer to
the first question regarding the features that can signify post-truth political
discourse remains somewhat elusive. It is difficult to isolate features which
pertain exclusively to post-truth as opposed to any other type of political
discourse. Still, one could easily identify that the use of self- and other
positioning occurs in political speeches and debates, along with the
associated pronominal referents and the types of moves employed by the
various political actors (cf. Berlin, 2012; forthcoming).

It can also be claimed that the very nature of political speeches and debates
is, by design, pragmatically embedded with emotionally charged topics,
especially given that the underlying pragmatic act of CONVINCING or

PERSUADING may require a heightened sense of engagement in order to rally support for the candidate (as in a campaign speech) and win voters away from an opponent (as in a debate) by making oneself appear more competent (1st order positioning) and, directly or indirectly, making one's opponent appear less competent or even incompetent ([2nd] 3rd order positioning).

Perhaps the one apparent difference between post-truth and traditional political discourse lies between the two types of discourse, speech versus debate. There is no challenge to claims made in speeches, whereas in a debate, the pragmatic upshot of the interaction goes against expected norms. In post-truth politics, false claims delivered as "truth" tend to be accepted as fact or simply ignored by the overhearing audience (i.e., the voters) as unimportant or irrelevant to their interests, even when factual challenges are presented by the opponent. From a pragmatic standpoint, this result shouldn't obtain. Earlier work in pragmatics has asserted that claims made by political actors which are later found to be false should have a detrimental effect on the individual who made the false claims. That is, when the falsity is discovered, an anticipated negative backlash should lead to a loss of support for the speaker. This has not been the case with Donald Trump and his staunchest supporters, either before or after the 2016 election. Thus, one potentially defining feature of post-truth political discourse is that it doesn't adhere to the normal expectations in pragmatics, nor to the general rules of communication. Consider, for example, that a speech act found to be infelicitous should fail and that a violation of one of the supermaxims of the Cooperative Principle should lead to the perception that the speaker is uncooperative and ultimately even untrustworthy. However, this presents an analytical conundrum since the identification of an untruth cannot necessarily be identified at the time of the utterance, but only after time has passed and outcomes can be witnessed.

In response to the second and third research questions, the specific moves (I-R-F) and their concomitant functions and positionings identified in the research, as well as the larger structures or patternings which occur in interactions (see Table 1.2), may hold a key to the recognition and understanding of post-truth political discourse. It is worth noting that the data obtained in the current study of false claims did not deviate from the strategies and their concomitant functions that have been identified. Further investigation will be necessary, however, to determine that the patterning is unique to post-truth and not other types of political discourse, especially if these moves and the structures in which they occur are meant to be defining in terms of ongoing research in post-truth politics.

References

Alterman, E. (2004). *When presidents lie: A history of official deception and its consequences.* New York: Viking.

Austin, J. L. (1962). *How to do things with words.* Oxford: Clarendon Press.

BBC News. (2016, November 16). "Post-truth" declared word of the year. Retrieved November 6, 2019, from https://www.bbc.com/news/uk-37995600.

Bakhtin, M. M. (1981). *The dialogic imagination: Four essays* (Ed. M. Holmquist). Austin: University of Texas Press.

Berlin, L. N. (2005). Media manipulation. In A. Betten & M. Dannerer (Eds.), *Dialogue analysis IX. Dialogue in literature and the media: Selected papers from the 9th IADA conference, Salzburg 2003–Part II: Media* (pp. 173-182). Tübingen: Max Niemeyer Verlag.

Berlin, L. N. (2007). Cooperative conflict and evasive language: The case of the 9-11 Commission hearings. In A. Fetzer (Ed.), *Context and appropriateness: Micro meets macro* (pp. 176–215). Amsterdam/Philadelphia: John Benjamins.

Berlin, L. N. (2008). "I think, therefore…": Commitment in political testimony. *Journal of Language and Social Psychology, 27* (4), 372–383.

Berlin, L. N. (2011a). Redundancy and markers of belief in the discourse of political hearings. *Language Sciences, 33* (2), 268-279.

Berlin, L. N. (2011b). Fighting words: Hybrid discourse and discourse processes. In A. Fetzer & E. Oishi (Eds.), *Context and contexts* (pp. 41–65). Amsterdam/Philadelphia: John Benjamins. DOI: 10.1075/pbns.209.04ber.

Berlin, L. N. (2011c). El modelo multinivel de contexto: un marco para explorar la manipulación del lenguaje y la manera en que lo mediático y lo político se fusionan en un discurso híbrido. *Discurso & Sociedad, 5* (1), 9-40.

Berlin, L. N. (2012). The making of a new American revolution or a wolf in sheep's clothing: "It's time to reload." In L. N. Berlin & A. Fetzer (Eds.), *Dialogue in politics* (pp. 167-192). Amsterdam/Philadelphia: John Benjamins.

Berlin, L. N. (2015). Pragmatic strategies for follow-ups in US political debates. In A. Fetzer, E. Weizman, & L. N. Berlin (Eds.), *The dynamics of political discourse: Forms and functions of follow-ups* (pp. 87-107). Amsterdam/Philadelphia: John Benjamins.

Berlin, L. N. (forthcoming). Positioning the voices of conflict: Language manipulation in the Diálogos de Paz. In I. Chiluwa (Ed.), *Discourses of conflict and conflict resolution.* Amsterdam/Philadelphia: John Benjamins.

Berlin, L. N., & Prieto-Mendoza, M. A. (2014). Evidential embellishment in political debates during US campaigns. *Intercultural Pragmatics, 11* (3), 389-409.

Blake, A. (2016a, September 26). The first Trump-Clinton presidential debate transcript, annotated. Retrieved May 15, 2017, from https://www.washingtonpost.com/news/the-fix/wp/2016/09/26/the-firsttrump-clinton-presidential-debate-transcript-annotated/?utm_term=.b40b9cb79c4e.

Blake, A. (2016b, October 19). The final Trump-Clinton debate transcript, annotated. Retrieved May 15, 2017, from https://www.washingtonpost.com/news/the-fix/wp/2016/10/19/the-final-trump-clinton-debate-transcript-annotated/?utm_term=.a8c04ce3a8b9.

Brown, P., & Levinson, S. C. (1987). *Politeness: Some universals in language usage.* Cambridge: Cambridge University Press.

Chouliaraki, L., & Fairclough, N. (1999). *Discourse in late modernity: Rethinking critical discourse analysis.* Edinburgh: Edinburgh University Press.

Davies, B., & Harré, R. (1990). Positioning: The discursive production of selves. *Journal for the Theory of Social Behavior, 20* (1), 43-63.

The Economist (2016, September 10). The post-truth world: Yes, I'd lie to you. *The Economist,* 17-20.

Farley, R. (2016, October 10). FactChecking the Second Presidential Debate. Retrieved May 20, 2017, from https://www.factcheck.org/2016/10/factchecking-the-secondpresidential-debate/.

Geertz, C. (1983). *Local knowledge* (3rd ed.). San Francisco: Basic Books.

Goffman, E. (1974). *Frame analysis.* Boston: Northeastern University Press.

Goffman, E. (1981). *Forms of talk.* Philadelphia: University of Pennsylvania.

Gore, D., Kiely, E., Jackson, B., Robertson, L., Farley, R., Schipani, V., Gross, Z., Wang, J., & Wallace, C. (2016, October 20). FactChecking the Final Presidential Debate. Retrieved May 20, 2017, from https://www.factcheck.org/2016/10/factchecking-the-final-presidential-debate-2/.

Grice, H. P. (1975). Logic and conversation. In P. Cole & J. L. Morgan (Eds.), *Speech acts: Syntax and semantics, Vol. 3* (pp. 41-58). New York: Academic.

Halliday, M. A. K. (1978). *Language as social semiotic: The social interpretation of language and meaning.* London: Edward Arnold.

Halliday, M. A. K. (1984). Language as code and language as behavior: A systemic-functional interpretation of the nature and ontogenesis of dialogue. In R. P. Fawcett, M. A. K. Halliday, S. M. Lamb, & A. Makkai (Eds.), *The semiotics of culture and language: Volume I: Language as social semiotic* (pp. 3-35). London and Wolfeboro, NH: Frances Pinter.

Harré, R., & van Langenhove, L. (1991). Varieties of positioning. *Journal for the Theory of Social Behaviour, 21* (4), 393-407.

Harré, R., & van Langenhove, L. (Eds.) (1999). *Positioning theory: Moral contexts of international action.* Oxford: Blackwell.

Hymes, D. (1972). Models of interaction of language and social life. In J. J. Gumperz & D. Hymes (Eds.), *Directions in sociolinguistics: The ethnography of communication* (pp. 35-71). New York: Holt, Rinehart and Winston.

Kessler, G., & Lee, M. Y. H. (2016a, September 27). Fact-checking the first Clinton-Trump presidential debate. Retrieved May 20, 2017, from https://www.washingtonpost.com/gdpr-consent/?destination=%2fnews%2ffact-checker%2fwp%2f2016%2f09%2f27%2ffact-checking-the-firstclinton-trump-presidential-debate%2f%3f.

Kessler, G., & Lee, M. Y. H. (2016b, October 20). Fact-checking the third Clinton-Trump presidential debate. Retrieved May 20, 2017, from https://www.washingtonpost.com/gdpr-consent/?destination=%2fnews%2ffact-checker%2fwp%2f2016%2f10%2f20%2ffact-checking-the-third-clinton-trump-presidential-debate%2f%3futm_term%3d.a3fe5c8b07c6&utm_term=.a3fe5c8b07c6.

Keyes, R. (2004). *The post-truth era: Dishonesty and deception in contemporary life.* New York: St. Martin's.

Lakoff, R. T. (1990). *Talking power: The politics of language.* San Francisco: Basic Books.

Lakoff, R. T. (2000) *The language war.* Berkeley, CA: University of California Press.

Malinowski, B. (1923). The problem of meaning in primitive languages. In C. K. Odgen & I. A. Richards (Eds.) *The meaning of meaning* (pp. 296-336). New York: Harcourt, Brace and World, Inc.

McAllister, I. (2016-04-05). Candidates and voting choice. *Oxford Research Encyclopedia of Politics.* Retrieved 4 Feb. 2018, from http://politics.oxfordre.com/view/10.1093/acrefore/9780190228637.001.0001/acrefore-9780190228637-e-73.

McKinney, M. & Warner, B. (2013). Do presidential debates matter? Examining a decade of campaign debate effects. *Argumentation and Advocacy, 49,* 238-258. DOI: 10.1080/00028533.2013.11821800.

Mey, J. L. (2001). *Pragmatics: An introduction (2nd ed.).* Malden, MA: Blackwell Publishing.

Minow, N. N., & LaMay, C. L. (2008). *Inside the presidential debates.* Chicago /London: University of Chicago Press.

The New York Times (2016, October 10). Transcript of the second debate. Retrieved May 20, 2017, from https://www.nytimes.com/2016/10/10/us/politics/transcript-seconddebate.html?_r=0.

Peters, G., & Woolley, J. T. (2016a, July 21). Donald J. Trump: Address Accepting the Presidential Nomination at the Republican National Convention in Cleveland, Ohio–July 21, 2016. Retrieved May 15, 2017, from http://www.presidency.ucsb.edu/ws/?pid=117935.

Peters, G., & Woolley, J. T. (2016b, July 28). Hillary Clinton: Address Accepting the Presidential Nomination at the Democratic National Convention in Philadelphia, Pennsylvania–July 28, 2016. Retrieved May 15, 2017, from http://www.presidency.ucsb.edu/ws/?pid=118051.

Prieto-Mendoza, M. A. (2020). Positioning in the peace process: Stance during the Colombian Peace Dialogues. In L. N. Berlin (Ed.), *Positioning and stance in political discourse: The individual, the party, and the party line,* (pp. 31-53). Wilmington, DE: Vernon Press.

Qiu, L. (2016a, September 27). Fact-checking the first presidential debate. Retrieved May 20, 2017, from https://www.politifact.com/truth-o-meter/article/2016/sep/27/trump-clinton-firstdebate-fact-checks/.

Qiu, L. (2016b, October 9). Fact-checking the second presidential debate. Retrieved May 20, 2017, from https://www.politifact.com/truth-o-meter/article/2016/oct/09/fact-checks-secondpresidential-debate/.

Roberts, D. (2010-04-01). Post-truth politics. *The Grist*. Retrieved 1 Oct. 2016, from http://grist.org/article/2010-03-30-post-truth-politics/.

Sbisà, M. (2002). Speech acts in context. *Language in Communication, 22,* 421–436.

Searle, J. R. (1969). *Speech acts.* Cambridge: Cambridge University Press.

Sinclair, J., & Coulthard, M. (1975). *Towards an analysis of discourse.* Oxford: Oxford University Press.

Tesich, S. (1992). A government of lies. *The Nation, 1* (12), 6.

van Dijk, T. A. (2003). Critical discourse analysis. In D. Schiffrin, D. Tannen, & H. E. Hamilton (Eds.), *The handbook of discourse analysis* (pp. 352-371). Oxford: Blackwell Publishing.

Warner, B., & McKinney, M. (2013). To unite and divide: The polarizing effect of presidential debates. *Communication Studies, 64,* 508-527. DOI: 10.1080/10510974.2013.832341.

Wittgenstein, L. (1958). *Philosophical investigations (2nd ed.).* Oxford: Blackwell.

Chapter 2

Positioning in the Peace Process:
The Colombian Peace Dialogues

Maria Alejandra Prieto-Mendoza[1]
University of Illinois at Chicago, United States

Abstract

Since the beginning of the peace process between the *Fuerzas Armadas Revolucionarias de Colombia, ejército del pueblo* (FARC) and the Colombian government under Juan Manuel Santos, each side has presented a series of public broadcasts to disseminate information to the Colombian people about the progress being made during the negotiations. This chapter compares results from an earlier study of the first public announcements to two subsequent sets of broadcasts selected from near the midpoint and the end of the Peace Dialogues in order to observe whether the early patterns found were maintained, modified, or discarded through the process. The earlier study (Berlin, 2015; forthcoming) used Positioning Theory (Harré & van Langenhove, 1991; 1999) to analyze how the two political entities positioned themselves and their counterparts in relation to the listening audience. The present study uses the Multilayered Model of Context framework (Berlin, 2007; 2011a; 2011b) and Positioning Theory; the analysis also shows how the broadcasts ultimately served to advance the political platforms of each side through their positioning, attempting to convince the public that they were more aligned with the people the other side.

1. Introduction

According to Eisenhart and Johnstone (2008), "discourse can be viewed as a collection of linguistic choices, choices about how to produce a particular utterance or text and choices about how to interpret what was spoken or written ... Each of these choices is strategic in that it represents a way of viewing the world that is valued by the discourse producer" (p. 54).

---

[1] I'd like to express my deepest thanks to Lawrence N. Berlin and Ana Patricia Muñoz Restrepo for their helpful comments in the revision of this chapter.

Accordingly, it is expected that utterances generated as a scripted summary of events, especially when made by opposing parties during a negotiation to negotiate peace, will likely represent the individual perspectives of the respective side.

Furthermore, every discourse choice made has the potential to resonate within a community of practice wherein participants share cultural norms (Eckert, 1988). The choices contain sets of values and visions which the speakers embed in their utterances, and which the hearers receive, assuming the communication is effectively transmitted. The imposition of these sets of values and visions can also emerge as effective speakers attempt to transmit their own ideologies, thereby manipulating language to achieve specific ends (cf. Berlin, 2015; forthcoming). These types of strategically created texts are constructed "in a specific social context" (Halliday, 1978, p. 265). Hence, language manipulation becomes a political practice that, in time, may boost or diminish any discourse and the identities formed by them (Howarth, Norval, & Stavrakakis, 1998). Taking into account how loaded a political text can be, language manipulation in political discourse wields power and is best studied through the lens of Critical Discourse Analysis (CDA).

CDA studies have shown the high level of control a speaker can maintain over the entire communication (Bolivar, 2005; Charteris-Black, 2012; Filardo-Llamas, 2013; Gavriely-Nuri, 2010; Romero-Trillo & Maguire, 2011; Valdeón García, 2009). In this regard, van Dijk (1999) explains that the control a speaker has on the discourse can be observed in the influence that not only the context, but also every linguistic structure has. In the case of the two parties involved in the Colombian Peace Dialogues, the FARC and the Colombian government have historically portrayed themselves as acting for the good of the people, positioning themselves positively while positioning their counterpart negatively. One of the ways each party has attempted to achieve this goal is "[i]nfluir o controlar para nuestro interés, la interpretación de enunciados" [to influence or control the interpretation of statements for our interests] (Olave, 2013, p. 341). This interpretation of statements is the particular goal each party aims to achieve so that the hearers will interpret the discourse according to the intended mean of the speaker.

Van Dijk (2006) refers to the way that discourse has the power to boost or attenuate the viewpoint of each participant:

> This strategy may operate at all levels, generally in such a way that our good things are emphasized and our bad things de-emphasized, and the opposite for the others–whose bad things will be enhanced, and whose good things will be mitigated, hidden or forgotten. (p. 126)

During these attempts to influence or control, each party also embeds language to communicate their political agenda and promote their ideology. Thus, every message has the potential to unconsciously tell the speaker how to think. Indeed,

> ideologies are not any kind of socially shared beliefs, such as sociocultural knowledge or social attitudes, but they are more fundamental or axiomatic because they have the capacity to control and organize other socially shared beliefs. (p. 116)

Since the beliefs may not be shared, the communicative goal of inculcating an ideology requires that each party creates a particular model of context.

> *Los modelos de contexto son objetos cognitivos o representaciones mentales de episodios comunicativos, en cuyo proceso de construcción los participantes–de diferentes modos–seleccionan aquellas propiedades visibles y no visibles que son discursivamente relevantes para definir la situación comunicativa.* [The models of context are cognitive objects or mental representations about communicative episodes, in which the participants–in different ways–select those discursively relevant properties, visible and invisible, in order to define the communicative situation.]

(Olave, 2013, p. 341)

Once the communicative situation is defined by the hearer, the selective work done by the speaker can be recognized and, in the case of an open and willing hearer, inculcated. Focusing on the process of meaning-making as dynamic and constructed, then, Positioning Theory (Harrè & van Langenhove, 1991; 1999) is informative as it provides a way to understand how speakers evolve and transform through the discourse. The theory provides a framework which allows the analyst to describe and explain how a speaker can align with or distance himself from an interlocutor.

Halliday (1978) and van Dijk (1999) both highlight the importance that context has on the language use in discourse to reference commonly shared sociocultural norms. Therefore, to conduct the CDA, the Multilayered Model of Context (MMC) (Berlin, 2007; 2011a; 2011b) was chosen to situate the language within its cultural context and allow for the incorporation of Positioning Theory. In Figure 1, the MMC is presented as a framework that defines the concept of context broadly, identifying four different levels.

Going beyond other analytic frameworks, the MMC includes (a) the extrasituational context, which offers insight into how participants interpret the discourse. Connecting diachronic and synchronic influences which shape the discourse make the communication relevant to the hearers. This level, which connects to other levels of discourse in what has been referred to as the "analysis of the conjuncture" (Chouliaraki & Fairclough, 1999), is also critical to the analyst. As connections are made between historical and contemporary events which are meaningful to participants in the communicative event, they offer and allow for a deeper analysis of the discourse.

The model also incorporates (b) the situational context. Grounded in anthropological theory (Spradley, 1980), it is based on the premise that specific actors in specific places perform specific activities. Thus, by conducting an "analysis of the practice" (Chouliaraki & Fairclough, 1999) in which actors engage, the role that people take in the discourse is situated socially and culturally, and establishes prototypes which become recognizable to observers.

The final two levels of the MMC, (c) the linguistic context and (d) the interactional context, correspond to the typical considerations in the study of pragmatics (Mey, 2001). Thus, the notion of the pragmatic act which contains both textual and action elements–*what* interlocutors say and *how* they intend it–can also be mapped onto these first two levels of context. They are also associated with and separated along the lines of Saussure's (1923) concepts of *langue* and *parole* and Halliday's (1984) definitions of "language as code" versus "language as behavior." Berlin (2011a; 2011b) also aligns the interface of these two levels to where Chouliaraki and Fairclough (1999) define the space where the "analysis of the discourse" occurs.

Figure 2.1. Multilayered Model of Context

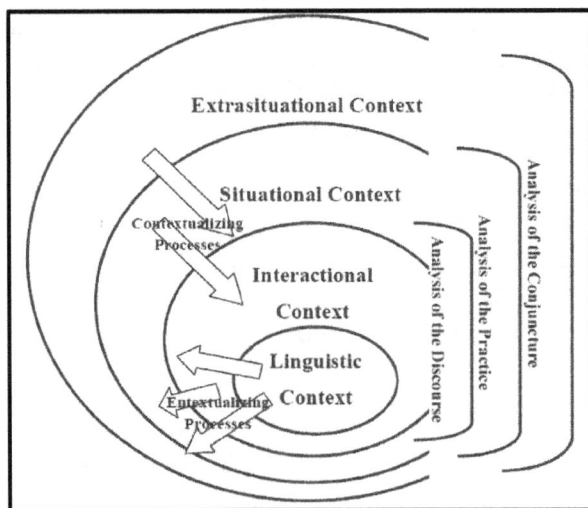

(Berlin, 2011a, p. 49)

Within a CDA, then, the MMC presents a fertile framework for the type of political discourse found in the public broadcasts made by the FARC and the Colombian government during the peace process. The power that words have during a communicative event, particularly a political one, and the capacity to change people's perspectives has been demonstrated (cf. Lakoff, 1990; 2000). Indeed, linguistic persuasion is the goal that politicians have in mind when delivering a speech to their audience or debating with their counterparts. Integrating Positioning Theory (Harré & van Langenhove, 1999), then, into the analysis of the discourse reveals the way actors position themselves in order to achieve their communicative goal (e.g., persuasion, transmission of ideology). Furthermore, the theory discloses the way parties may change their position several times during the same discourse. The dynamic nature of the theory within the MMC framework also helps in describing and explaining the linguistic behavior of the FARC and the Colombian Government.

Berlin (2015, forthcoming) analyzed the positioning exhibited by the FARC and the Colombian government during the first round of speeches in the Colombian Peace Dialogues.[2] The two political entities present their respective transmissions to the Colombian public; a relationship between their first, second, and third order positioning aligned with their situational and extrasituational contexts. Thus, the FARC presented a "revolutionary discourse" that portrayed them as inclusive and on the side of the audience. The Colombian government, contrastively, tended to use an exclusionary type of other positioning with the audience, presenting themselves in a hegemonic, "in control" positioning throughout the broadcast.

Remembering that each political side's main goal in political positioning is to gain influence, such that the hearers ultimately accept their political ideology (Berlin, 2015; forthcoming), it can be said that "a position in a conversation … is a metaphorical concept through reference to which a person's 'moral' and personal attributes as a speaker are compendiously collected" (Harré & van Langenhove, 1999, p. 17). Consequently, the power that words have cannot be understated, including their ability to assign rights and/or duties to others during any communicative interaction (Harré & Moghaddam, 2003).

Ultimately, seeking to understand the way a speaker can transmit, assign, or change people's roles during discourse through his positioning, and the way that politicians constantly make use of persuasion in order to win sympathizers, we commence with the study at hand. Starting with the results found previously in Berlin (2015, forthcoming), two additional sets of public

---

[2] Public statements delivered at the end of the first cycle of talks were recorded in Havana, Cuba on November 28 and 29, 2012.

statements presented during the Colombian Peace Dialogues were selected and examined to respond to the following questions:

1. Do the political entities of the Colombian Peace Dialogues continue to perform in the same way throughout the entire peace process?
2. Do they continue to use the same pragmatic strategies identified in an earlier study (Berlin, 2015; forthcoming) throughout the peace process? If not, what are the strategies used by each side?
3. How does the strategy selected by each party unfold in terms of positioning?

2. Methodology

2.1. Texts

In order to investigate the questions, public statements broadcast by the FARC and the Colombian government were selected for comparison, representing a total of 6 separate texts. These statements had been recorded and transcribed in the original Spanish, and made available online (*Humanas Colombia*, n.d.). As stated previously, in order to address the first question, I started with the two initial statements delivered by the two political entities studied in Berlin (2015; forthcoming). To explore the breadth of the dialogues during the peace process, a set of two additional broadcasts from the midpoint of the process (Cycle 22) and a set of two from the end (Cycle 45) were chosen for analysis. These paired broadcasts were deemed to be representative and provided fertile ground for study.

2.2. Levels of analyses

2.2.1. Extrasituational context

In order to better understand the multiple levels of context that influenced the Peace Dialogues between the FARC and the Colombian government, this study made use of the Multilayered Model of Context (Berlin, 2007; 2011a; 2011b).

Beginning with the analysis of the conjecture and the extrasituational context which informs it, it is necessary to take into consideration the way this event unfolded over the years to create the appropriate context for understanding. August 2016 marks the end of the Colombian conflict, which has lasted for more than 60 years. The origins of this conflict have been traced to a political rivalry between the liberals and the conservatives. Their vying for power created great dissatisfaction among peasant farmers with the way the government was legislating various issues, especially land rights. The mounting discontent reached its apex in 1948. Upon the assassination of the liberal presidential candidate, Jorge Eliecer Gaitan, violence broke out in the capital, Bogotá–an event remembered as *El Bogotazo*. Many people were killed and buildings were burned in the center of the city. However, *El Bogotazo* was only the beginning of a period that lasted for more than 10 years, known as *La Epoca de la Violencia* ("the Age of Violence").

During *La Epoca de la Violencia*, some people's negative feelings toward the government continued to escalate, resulting in the formation of armed vigilante groups, later referred to as *guerillas*. One of the most renowned guerilla groups is the *Fuerzas Armadas Revolucionarias de Colombia, ejército del pueblo* (FARC). The FARC have been one of the main participants in the ongoing conflict with the Colombian government. In 2012, however, the FARC agreed to open peace dialogues with the government under President Juan Manuel Santos. During the negotiations (from 2012 to 2016), the two parties addressed different points on the agenda they had set; each period of talk was referred to as a "cycle." At the beginning or at the end of each cycle, both the FARC and the government made a public statement to the Colombian population to inform them about the status of the peace process. Although the process officially ended with the signing of a peace agreement by both parties, the conflict has left more than 200,000 dead in the country.

Moving from the diachronic to the synchronic influences on the discourse, it can also be observed that there was a time leading up to the commencement of the Peace Dialogues when the government made the announcements about what both parties had agreed upon in order to engage in discourse with the idea of hopefully finding peace. Four stages were posited for the completion of the process:

(a) *Los acercamientos secretos* [secret approaches]
(b) *La concreción de los acuerdos* [the formalization of the agreements]
(c) *La refrendación* [endorsement]
(d) *La implementación de acuerdos* [the implementation of the agreements]

The formalization of the agreements was the moment when all the terms had been discussed and a final agreement was reached. The agreement, as it exists today, comprised approximately 50 cycles of talk.[3] As previously mentioned, both parties issued a public at the beginning and/or at the end of each cycle during which they shared their respective versions of the progress or lack thereof being made in the negotiations for peace. Details of the various elements of the process, including community forums and public exhibitions, can be found online at *Humanas Colombia* (n.d.).

Figure 2.2. Extrasituational context (analysis of the conjuncture)

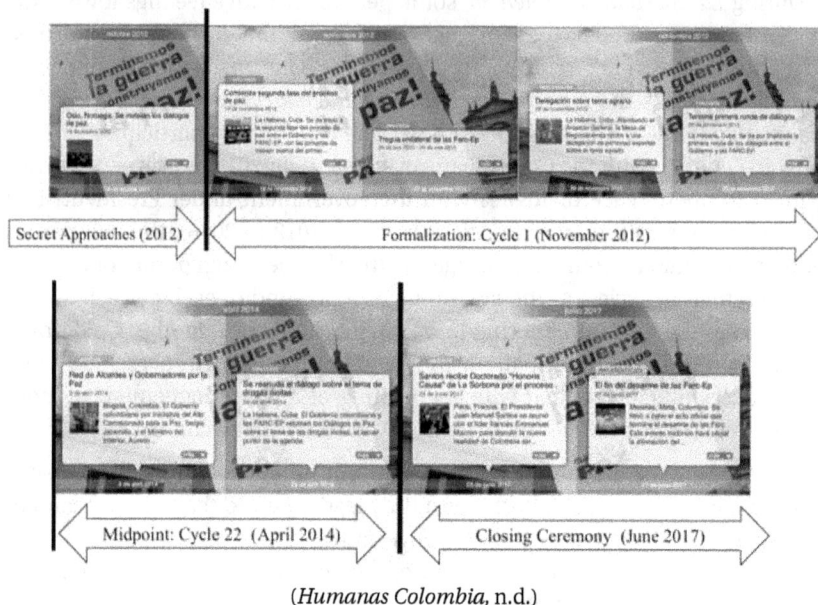

(*Humanas Colombia*, n.d.)

Figure 2.2 gives a sample of events which occurred at different points within the peace process (i.e., synchronic). The arrows denote the beginning and end of a specific period (e.g., "Formalization: 1st Cycle"). Each of the periods identified in Figure 2.2 was followed by a televised public statement, which is also available on the web. Additionally, this chronogram also presents a summary of the different activities–in addition to the negotiations–that were taking place at the same time as the talks taking place in Havana. The activities included public events that took place across all the regions of Colombia; their purpose was to enable the people to "reflect on what had transpired in the country over the 70-year period ... to address the issues of memory and move toward reconciliation as a vital part of the peace process"

---

[3] This is an "approximate" number because, after Cycle 45, there appear some discrepancies in the ordering as different sources that shared the information presented the same cycle in a different order or on a different date.

(Berlin, forthcoming). There were also "mesas regionales" [regional tables] where the public could present themes for the dialogues, without any influence either from the government or from the FARC.

2.2.2. Situational context

Figure 2.3 offers a representation of the situational context. It is at this stage that we can explore the analysis of the practice. As such, a unidirectional transmission of information can be observed. The speakers or actors, in this case the spokesperson for the FARC and the spokesperson for the Colombian government, were engaged in the activity of presenting a public statement in each of the cycles analyzed for this study to the Colombian population. As the statements were televised, the location was a closed studio; therefore, although the public was addressed in real-time, there was no possibility for interaction between the hearing audience and the spokespeople.

Figure 2.3. Situational context (analysis of the practice)

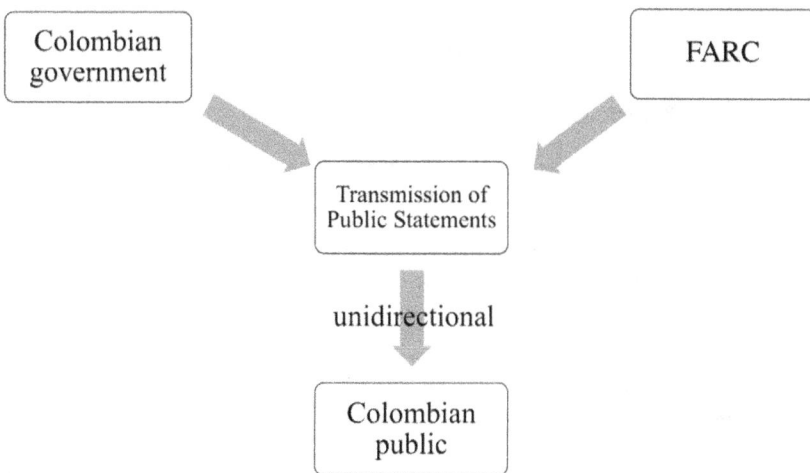

2.2.3. Interactional context

To begin the analysis of the discourse, this study integrated Positioning Theory (Harré, Moghaddam, Cairnie, Rothbart, & Sabat, 2009; Harré & van Langenhove, 1991; 1999; Moghaddam & van Langenhove, 2003). It fits within a pragmatic analysis by focusing on the way speakers use words (and discourse of all types) to locate themselves and others in the discourse. Furthermore, Positioning Theory allows us to explore how "it is with words that we ascribe rights and claim them for ourselves and place duties on others" (Moghaddam & Harré, 2010, p. 3).

Van Langenhove and Harré (1999), for instance, talk about the positioning triangle in regards to the background conditions required for any conversational situation. As seen in Figure 2.4, the social force, similar to the illocutionary force of the utterance (Sbisá, 2002; Searle, 1969), and the storyline, which can be described as the content and distribution of rights and duties among participants, work together with the position. Within positioning, we find three orders, aligned with the concept of "person" in communication (i.e., first, second, and third person, corresponding to the speaker/emitter of the communication, the hearer/receiver of the communication, and any other outside the immediate communication). First order positioning aligns with the way we present ourselves within discourse; second order positioning is the way we position the intended hearers or audience, which can be through direct or indirect reference. Finally, there is third order positioning, which is the way in which the speaker positions others outside the communication and for whom the communication is not intended.[4]

Figure 2.4. Positioning triangle

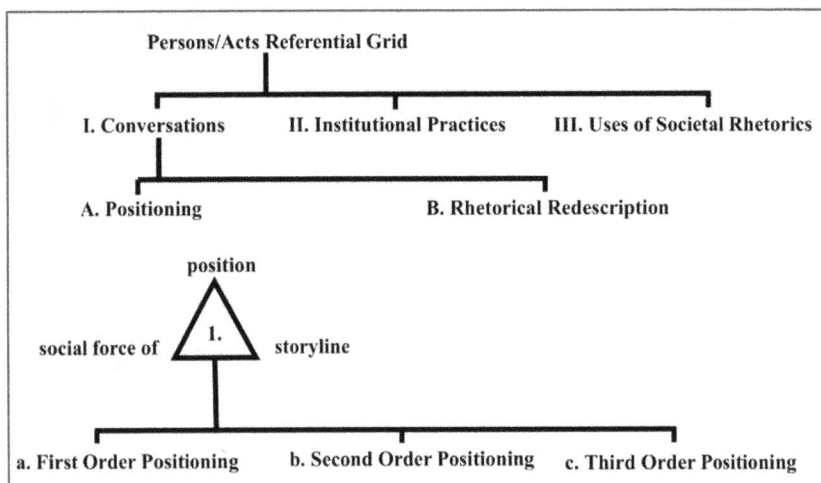

(Berlin, 2015, based on Harré & van Langenhove, 1999)

2.3. Findings and discussion

The texts analyzed come from the public statements presented at the midpoint (Cycle 22) and the closing ceremony of the Colombian Peace

---

[4] cf. Bell (1984) for a discussion of "overhearers" who may or may not be part of the targeted recipients.

Dialogues. These data were compared with texts from Cycle 1 explored in an earlier study (Berlin, 2015; forthcoming) to explore the questions presented at the end of Section 1.[5]

In excerpt (1), taken from Cycle 22, the spokesperson for the Colombian government begins by integrating an inclusive "we" form with "*Finalizamos en el día de hoy un ciclo de conversaciones,*" "*informamos* en el comunicado conjunto," and "*hemos* avanzado en la construcción de acuerdos."

(1)

Finalizamos [1st O][1st PP-incl] *en el día de hoy un ciclo de conversaciones en el que tal como lo informamos* [1st O][1st PP-incl] *en el comunicado conjunto ya conocido hemos avanzado* [1st O][3rd PP-incl] *en la construcción de acuerdos en un tema muy sensible para Colombia y para la comunidad internacional como lo es la solución del problema de las drogas ilícitas.*

We have ended another cycle of conversations today which, as we have informed you in the joint statement, we have moved on towards the construction of agreements in a very sensitive topic for Colombia and the international community, as it is the solution to the illicit drugs program.

While none of the references appear inclusive of the Colombian people, they do at least include the FARC, as highlighted in the reference to the "comunicado conjunto." However, the inclusive use quickly devolves after the opening, as seen in (2):

(2)

Por otra parte, al comienzo de este ciclo de conversaciones el jefe de la delegación de las Farc se refirió [3rd O][3rd PS] *públicamente a la Comisión de la Verdad, asunto que se ha discutido en la Mesa de Conversaciones.*

---

[5] All the excerpts from the texts are presented in the original Spanish, followed by an English translation.

El Gobierno no escamotea [1st O][3rd PS-excl] *la verdad del conflicto.*
Queremos [1st O][1st PP-excl], *por encima de todo, que esa verdad o*
esas verdades del conflicto–todas–afloren y se conozcan.

On the other hand, at the beginning of this cycle of talks, the head of
the FARC delegation referred publicly to the Truth Commission, an
issue that has been discussed at the Table of Conversations.

The Government does not spare the truth of the conflict. We want,
above all, that that truth or those truths of the conflict–all–emerge and
be known.

In the presentation of three points to resolve the illicit drug situation, the
government spokesman clearly separates the two sides in the discourse,
identifying "el jefe de la delegación de las FARC" [the head of the FARC
delegation] and "El Gobierno" [the government]. Thus, the "we" that follows,
beginning with "Queremos" [We want], and from that point forward, is
exclusive of the FARC and represents the government's perspective towards
the truth. At times, a hegemonic tone emerges, especially with regard to the
governmental desire to uncover the truth, indexing its hidden nature with
allusions to FARC's role–"se refirió públicamente" [referred publicly]–in an
alleged cover-up–"que esa verdad y esas verdades del conflicto–todas–afloren
y se conozcan" [that that truth and those truths of the conflict–all–emerge and
be known].

In excerpt (3), the government spokesman states that "Seguimos trabajando
sin descanso para pactar el fin del conflicto" [We continue working without
rest to come to an agreement on ending the conflict]. Though FARC is an
ostensive partner in bringing an end to the conflict, the positioning seems to
shift to being inclusive, but in an attempt to align themselves with the
Colombian people rather than the FARC. The relative clause "que nos abra esa
posibilidad de paz" [that could open for us the possibility for peace], albeit
from a hegemonic position, is strengthened in its realignment with the people
in the final relative clause, "que es el sueño más grande hoy de nuestro país"
[which is the biggest dream for our country today]. While this doesn't
necessarily exclude the FARC, without whose participation in the peace
process there would be no peace, it cannot be forgotten that many consider
the FARC, as well as other guerilla groups, as primarily responsible for the
ongoing unrest. Thus, the realization of the dream of peace, when presented
from the government's point of view, was only attainable because of the
public outcry and their own willingness to enter into a dialogue with the
FARC.

(3)

Seguimos trabajando [1st O][1st PP- excl] *sin descanso para pactar el fin del conflicto que nos abra* [1st O][1st PP-incl] *esa posibilidad de paz que es el sueño más grande hoy de nuestro país* [1st O][1st PP-incl]

We continue working without rest to come to an agreement on ending the conflict that could open for us the possibility for peace, which is the biggest dream for our country today.

From the point of view of the FARC, excerpt (4) presents examples of first ordering position which are consistently inclusive of the Colombian people, but not the government. This excerpt, also from cycle 22, provides another example of FARC's demonstrated tendency to show themselves as being "one with the people" in their reference to the "logros" [achievements] which "nos dan optimismo" [make us optimistic] while "siempre poniendo los pies sobre base de realismo" [always trying to be grounded in realism]. In addition, (4) provides an example of first order positioning exclusive only to the FARC when they mention "el alto propósito que nos hemos trazado" [the high goal we have outlined for ourselves] in order to achieve peace.

(4)

Es un hecho que los logros nos dan optimismo [1st O][1st PP-incl] *siempre poniendo los pies sobre base de realismo pero con la determinación de hacer hasta lo imposible por alcanzar el alto propósito que nos hemos trazado* [1st O][1st PP-excl].

It is a fact that the present achievements make us optimistic, always trying to be grounded in realism, but with the determination to do everything including the impossible in order to achieve the high goal we have outlined for ourselves.

In (5), the second example from the FARC, there are instances of first ordering position using third person reference (i.e., FARC refer to themselves as "the FARC"), and, in an attempt to portray an intimate interaction between themselves and the public, they praise the actions of the Colombian people by referring to "el protagonismo creciente del movimiento popular en la definición de los destinos de Colombia" [the increasing leading role of the popular movement in defining Colombia's destiny], claiming that they "exaltan sus reivindicaciones y asumen con determinación su llamada a recuperar la memoria colectiva" [exalt in your vindication and take up your call to recuperate the collective memory].

(5)

Por eso la FARC-ep saludan [1st O][1st PP-excl] *el protagonismo creciente del movimiento popular en la definición de los destinos de Colombia, exaltan* [1st O][1st PP-excl] *sus* [2nd O][3rd PP] *reivindicaciones y asumen* [1st O][1st PP-excl] *con determinación su llamada* [2nd O][3rd PP] *a recuperar la memoria colectiva … y a adelantar un proceso constituyente que con el concurso de todos y todas, junte la argamasa con la que se modelará el anhelado tratado de paz estable y duradero que necesita el país* [2nd O][3rd PS].

For that reason, the FARC-ep greet the increasing leading role of the popular movement in defining Colombia's destiny, [the FARC] exalt in your vindication and take up your call with determination to recuperate the collective memory … and to advance a constitutional process that, with everybody's participation, joins the mortar that will shape the long-awaited peace agreement, stable and lasting, that the country needs.

The evocative language used here also appears to be a call to recover a truth that may have been clouded or completely lost; while it need not be interpreted as an indictment against the Colombian government–although it could be an indirect third order, other positioning–it is, at the very least, an attempt to get the public to recognize a need for FARC in the future of Colombia in order to achieve a "tratado de paz estable y duradero que necesita el país" [peace agreement, stable and lasting, that the country needs].

The second set of analyzed excerpts come from closing ceremonies speeches presented by both parties. This last set of broadcasts is very interesting because it presents a totally different point of view from both the Colombian government and the FARC.

Excerpt (6) presents an example of the Colombian Government using first order positioning, which appears to be all-inclusive. The reference to "abrimos la puerta a una sociedad más incluyente" [we open the door to a more inclusive society] either intends to include the FARC in the "we" in "abrimos" [we open] or as part of the "sociedad más incluyente" [more inclusive society]. The rhetoric at least maintains a possibility for a truly open and accepting democratic society when it states that "nadie tema por su integridad a consecuencia de sus ideas políticas" [no one worries about their integrity because of their political ideas].

(6)

Bajo el telón de fondo de la reconciliación, abrimos [1st O][1st PP- incl] *la puerta a una sociedad más incluyente en la que podamos reconocernos como colombianos* [1st O][1st PP- incl], *en la que nadie tema por su integridad a consecuencia de sus ideas políticas.* [1st O][3rd PP- incl]

Under the backdrop of reconciliation, we open the door to a more inclusive society in which we can recognize ourselves as Colombians, (a society) in which no one worries about their integrity because of their political ideas.

In the second excerpt from the government, (7), shows again first ordering position inclusive of the FARC, when they talk about the things they do and didn't do these past years, to obtain peace. Another stance that can be observed in this example is the presence of second order positioning for Colombia, showing how the government separates themselves from the population and show they, the FARC and the Government together, achieved this peace agreement for the Colombians.

(7)

No hemos hecho [1st O][1st PP- incl] *propiamente una negociación. No hemos cambiado* [1st O][1st PP- incl] *fusiles por convicciones. Estamos seguros* [1st O][1st PP- incl] *de haber logrado una hoja de ruta para Colombia* [2nd O][3rd PP].

In this almost 4 years, we have not precisely conducted a negotiation. We have not exchanged rifles for convictions. We are sure to have achieved a roadmap for Colombia.

The moments of separation are fewer, but they do exist. The speaker begrudgingly admits to a better existence since the commencement of the Peace Dialogues in (8) when he states:

(8)

Por cierto, a partir de los ceses de fuego unilaterales de las FARC [3rd O][3rd PP], *hemos vivido* [1st O][1st PP-incl] *los meses de menor confrontación militar en varias décadas.*

By the way, from the unilateral ceasefire of the FARC, we have experienced the months of least military confrontation in several decades.

The reference to the recent period that "hemos vivido" [we have experienced] is an inclusive "we" whereby the government aligns themselves with the public at the expense of the FARC (i.e., FARC aren't part of the inclusion).

The discourse presented by the FARC also makes use of a somewhat ambiguous first ordering positioning. Though the two sides were necessary for the negotiation of peace to be achieved, the reference in (9) to "hemos construido durante más de medio siglo de rebeldía" [we have built during more than half a century of rebellion] clearly suggests that they are positioning themselves as being the ones to deliver the peace to the people of Colombia. Similar to their style demonstrated elsewhere, (9) shows them talking about what they are giving to the Colombian people, and how this is now "un sueño colectivo" [a collective dream].

(9)

Hoy estamos entregando [1st O][1st PP-excl] *al pueblo colombiano* [2nd O][3rd PS] *la potencia transformadora que hemos construido* [1st O][1st PP-excl] *durante más de medio siglo de rebeldía para que con ella y la fuerza de la unión, empiece a edificar la sociedad del futuro, la de nuestro* [1st O][1st PP-incl] *sueño colectivo, con un santuario consagrado a la democracia, a la justicia social, a la soberanía y a las relaciones de hermandad y de respeto con todo el mundo* [2nd O][3rd PS].

Today we are giving the Colombian people the transformative power that we have built during more than half a century of rebellion so that with it and the strength of the union, it will begin to build the society of the future, that of our collective dream, with a sanctuary dedicated to the democracy, social justice, sovereignty and brotherhood and respect relations with everyone.

These efforts to position themselves as aligned with the public work discursively to achieve what the armed rebellion could not: a full reintegration into the Colombian society.

In (10), the last example from the FARC, we see another example of first order positioning, albeit exclusive, wherein the FARC leaves behind its revolutionary language, which has dotted much of their discourse and puts on a human face.

(10)

Confesamos [1st O][1st PP-excl] *que ha sido una construcción dura y llena de dificultades, con luces y tal vez con sombras, pero trabajada con el corazón lleno de amor por la patria y los pobres de Colombia* [2nd O][3rd PP].

We confess that it has been a hard construction and full of difficulties, with lights and perhaps with shadows, but worked with a heart full of love for the country and the poor of Colombia.

With "Confesamos que ha sido una construcción dura" [We confess that it has been a hard construction], the FARC offer a confession which can open the door for true reconciliation in a culture that understands the need to hear a confession in order to offer forgiveness.

The remainder of their public announcement offers greetings and reaches out to the various segments within Colombian society and the world beyond. But, as in the majority of their other statements, they make no direct reference to the Colombian government, with one exception. In the last sentence of their public statement, they name the negotiator from the government side by name and reinforce the religious references as they exclaim, "Del cónclave de La Habana ha surgido humo blanco, doctor Humberto de La Calle. Habemus Pacem, tenemos paz" [White smoke has emerged from the conclave of Havana, Dr. Humberto de La Calle. Habemus Pacem, we have peace].

2.4 Comparisons

Returning to the study of the opening statements (Berlin, 2015; forthcoming), the question investigated whether the political actors in the Peace Dialogues had performed as might be predicted in terms of positioning. That is, FARC was expected to demonstrate more first order positioning with an inclusive "we." Furthermore, it was predicted that their second order positioning would present a favorable portrayal of the public as they attempted to align themselves with the Colombian people in order to commence the path to reintegration into Colombian society. Their revolutionary discourse was also expected. In terms of the Colombian government, it was expected that there would be more first order positioning that used an exclusive "we," maintaining the appearance of a government that maintained control and had the upper hand, thus reinforcing their hegemonic position. As reported in the Berlin study, all these expectations were met.

Moving on to the comparison of the results found in Berlin (2015; forthcoming) with the current study, we can see in Figure 2.5 how the FARC positioning is represented from Cycle 1 to Cycle 22 to the closing.

Figure 2.5. FARC positioning

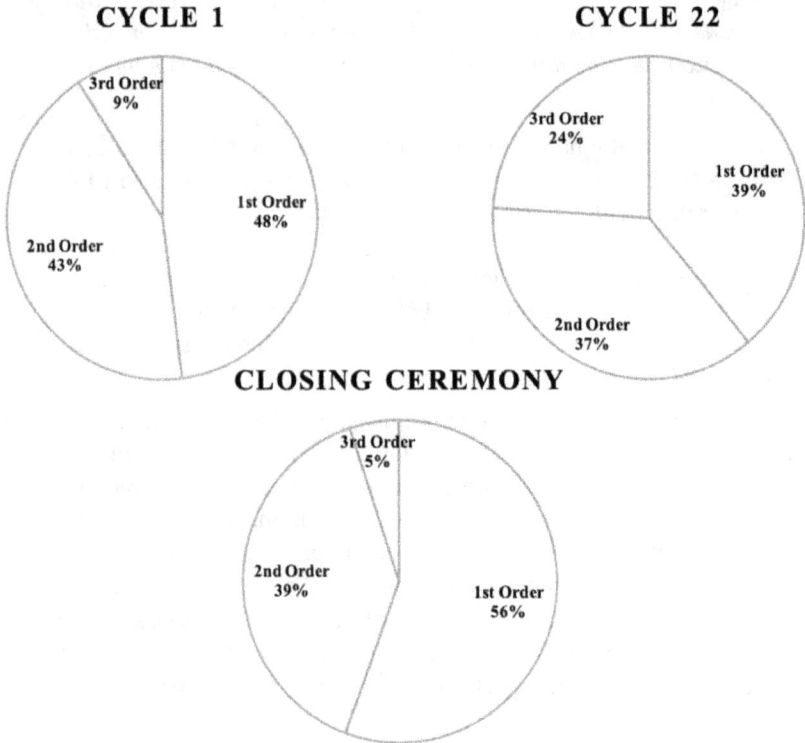

CYCLE 1

CYCLE 22

3rd Order 9%

1st Order 48%

2nd Order 43%

3rd Order 24%

1st Order 39%

2nd Order 37%

CLOSING CEREMONY

3rd Order 5%

2nd Order 39%

1st Order 56%

Of the pragmatic strategies identified, FARC exhibited a great degree of consistency in terms of the overall use of first, second, and third order positioning. Their first order positioning represented the majority of their positioning work (48% at time 1, 39% at time 2, and 56% at the closing). Additionally, their use of second order positioning (43%, 37%, and 39%, respectively) and third order positioning (9%, 24%, and 5%, respectively) was proportionally consistent throughout.

In the performance exhibited by the Colombian government, certain patterns emerged. Progressing from Cycle 1 to Cycle 22 to the Closing Ceremony, the proportions shifted: the higher use of first order positioning in Cycle 1 and the Closing Ceremony was replaced in Cycle 22 by second order positioning; third order positioning, however, was consistently the smallest proportion until the Closing Ceremony when there was no evidence of third order positioning at all. Figure 2.6 shows how the Colombian government's pragmatic performance played out over the course of the Peace Dialogues.

Figure 2.6. Government positioning

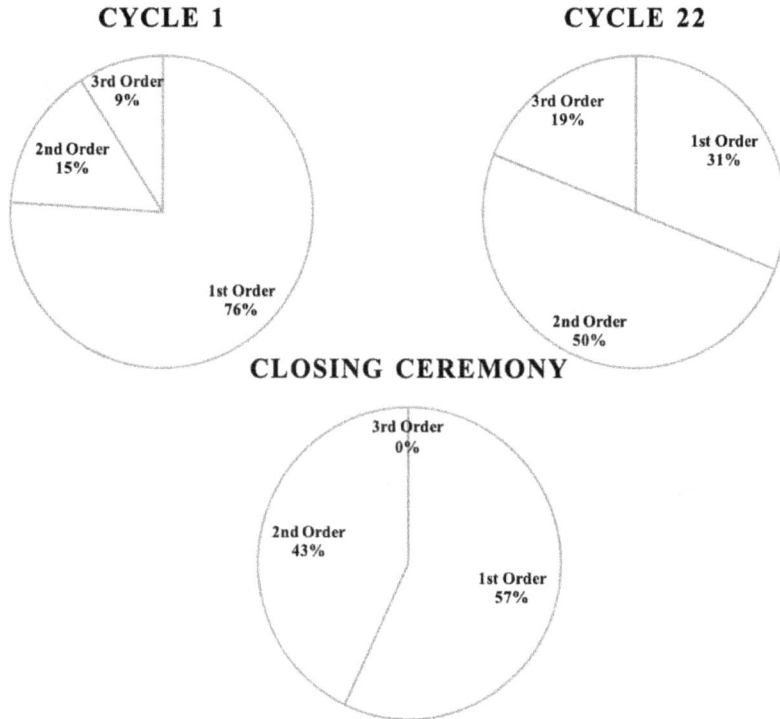

CYCLE 1

CYCLE 22

3rd Order 9%

2nd Order 15%

1st Order 76%

3rd Order 19%

1st Order 31%

2nd Order 50%

CLOSING CEREMONY

3rd Order 0%

2nd Order 43%

1st Order 57%

Their first order positioning was highest in Cycle 1 (76%), making a resurgence in the Closing Ceremony (57%). Their second order and third order positioning progressed in contrasting directions (15%, 50%, and 43%, respectively; 9%, 19%, and 0%, respectively).

In Figure 2.7, it becomes clear that there is a convergence between the performance of the two sides, particularly in terms of their first order positioning. Indeed, a higher presence of first ordering position inclusive of the other side emerges (i.e., the FARC referring to themselves, as well as the Colombian government, and *vice versa*). Having reached an agreement, this pragmatic patterning is perhaps to be expected, given that they did, in fact, reach agreement. This is not to say, however, that they moved closer together to each other, but rather that they both tended to move closer to their target: a compromise.

Figure 2.7. Closing ceremony first order positioning (inclusive vs. exclusive)

FARC   GOVERNMENT

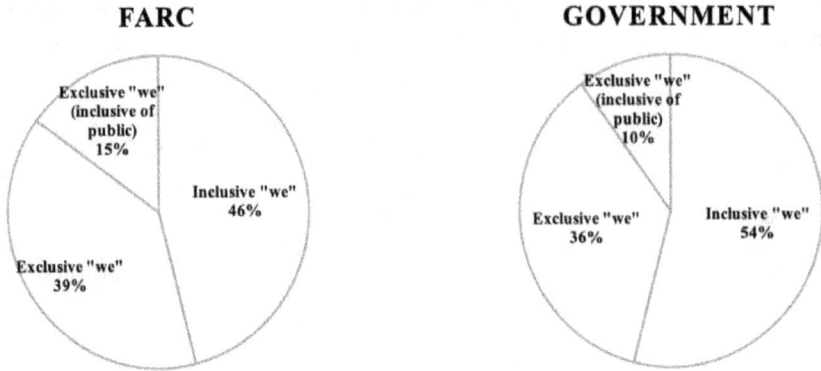

While there was still a high degree of exclusive first order positioning (39% and 36% by the respective sides) with a smaller degree of alignment with the Colombian people, especially on the part of the Colombian public (15% by FARC and 10% by the government), it can still be claimed that the pragmatic performances meet expectations. Berlin (2015; forthcoming) found that the FARC utilized strategies to move closer to reconciliation with the Colombian people in order to reintegrate into society; this is evident at all points analyzed and results in a change in strategy (e.g., allusions to the Catholic doctrine in the Closing Ceremony) to achieve the same ends through different means. From the government's side, while making concessions to achieve peace for the people, they maintain that they have been consistent in their efforts to arrive at an agreement on their own terms.

5. Conclusions

This study demonstrates how the Colombian government and the FARC performed consistently throughout a major part of the Peace Dialogues with proportions of first, second, and third order positioning emerging roughly unchanged. From the first cycle through the midpoint, the two sides also performed as expected in terms of employing similar pragmatic strategies to achieve their respective aims. The Colombian government presented themselves as powerful and in control in terms of not only the nation, but also the direction of the peace process. The FARC, taking into account their desire to reintegrate into Colombian society, similarly performed as expected: presenting themselves as one with the people. Their traditional revolutionary discourse, while expected, underscored their Marxist-Leninist roots and functioned to present them as being one with the people and struggling against the oppression of a capitalist regime.

As the two opposing sides approached a resolution, the final set of speeches at the closing ceremony came with a dramatic, yet expected change in positioning. At this culminating point, both parties presented themselves through first order positioning, favoring the first person plural, inclusive "we," speaking on behalf of both the FARC and the Government. Though "dramatic" in terms of representing a change in the direction that had been taken and maintained throughout a large part of the process, the "expected" is due to the logical move toward alignment as they reached an agreement on peace. Furthermore, the positioning at the exclusion of the Colombian people at the closing ceremony allowed both parties to share a common storyline: "We did this for you, Colombia."

References

Bell, A. (1984). Language style as audience design. *Language in Society, 13*, 145-204.

Berlin, L. N. (2007). Cooperative conflict and evasive language: The case of the 9-11 Commission Hearings. In A. Fetzer (Ed.), *Context and appropriateness* (pp. 167-199). Amsterdam/Philadelphia: John Benjamins.

Berlin, L. N. (2011a). Fighting words: Hybrid discourse and discourse processes. In A. Fetzer & E. Oishi (Eds.), *Context and contexts* (pp. 41–65). Amsterdam/Philadelphia: John Benjamins. DOI: 10.1075/pbns.209.04ber.

Berlin, L. N. (2011b). *El Modelo Multinivel de Contexto: un marco para explorar la manipulación del lenguaje y la manera en que lo mediático y lo político se fusionan en un discurso híbrido. Discurso & Sociedad, 5* (1), 9-40.

Berlin, L. N. (2015, October). *Positioning the voices of conflict: Language manipulation in the diálogos de paz.* Conference session presented at the 7th Dialogue Under Occupation (DUO VII) Conference, Porto Alegre, Brazil.

Berlin, L. N. (forthcoming). Positioning the voices of conflict: Language manipulation in the Diálogos de Paz. In I. Chiluwa (Ed.), *Discourses of conflict and conflict resolution.* Amsterdam/Philadelphia: John Benjamins.

Berlin, L. N., & Fetzer, A. (Eds.). (2012). *Dialogue in politics* (Vol. 18). John Benjamins Publishing.

Berlin, L. N., & Prieto-Mendoza, M. A. (2014). Evidential embellishment in political debates during US campaigns. *Intercultural Pragmatics, 11* (3), 389-409.

Bolívar, A. (2005). The president and the media. In A. Betten & M. Dannerer (Eds.), *Dialogue Analysis IX: Dialogue in literature and the media: Selected papers from the 9th IADA conference, Salzburg 2003–Part II: Media* (pp. 215-226). Tübingen: Max Niemeyer Verlag.

Charteris-Black, J. (2005). *Politicians and rhetoric: The persuasive power of metaphor.* Basingstoke/New York: Palgrave Macmillan.

Chouliaraki, L., & Fairclough, N. (1999). *Discourse in late modernity: Rethinking critical discourse analysis.* Edinburgh: Edinburgh University Press.

Eisenhart, C., & Johnstone, B. (2008). Introduction: Discourse analysis and rhetorical studies. In B. Johnstone & C. Eisenhart (Eds.), *Rhetoric in detail: Discourse analysis of rhetorical talk and text* (pp. 3-21). Amsterdam/Philadelphia: John Benjamins.

Eckert, P. (1988). Adolescent social structure and the spread of linguistic change. *Language in Society, 17*, 245-67.

Filardo-Llamas, L. (2013). "Committed to the ideals of 1916": The language of paramilitary groups: The case of the Irish Republican Army. *Critical Discourse Studies, 10* (1), 1-17. DOI: 10.1080/17405904.2012.736396.

Gavriely-Nuri, D. (2010). The idiosyncratic language of Israeli "peace": A cultural approach to critical discourse analysis (CCDA). *Discourse & Society, 21* (5), 565-585.

Goffman, E. (1955). On face-work: An analysis of ritual elements in social interaction. *Psychiatry, 18* (3), 213-231.

Halliday, M. A. K. (1978). *Language as social semiotic: The social interpretation of language and meaning.* London: Edward Arnold.

Halliday, M. A. K. (1984). Language as code and language as behavior: A systemic-functional interpretation of the nature and ontogenesis of dialogue. In R. P. Fawcett, M. A. K. Halliday, S. M. Lamb, & A. Makkai (Eds.), *The semiotics of culture and language: Volume I: Language as social semiotic* (pp. 3-35). London and Wolfeboro, NH: Frances Pinter.

Harré, R., & van Langenhove, L. (1991). Varieties of positioning. *Journal for the Theory of Social Behaviour, 21* (4), 393-407.

Harré, R., & Moghaddam, F. M. (Eds.). (2003). *The self and others: Positioning individuals and groups in personal, political, and cultural contexts.* Westport, CT: Praeger.

Harré, R., Moghaddam, F. M., Cairnie, T. P., Rothbart, D., & Sabat, S. R. (2009). Recent advances in Positioning Theory. *Theory & Psychology, 19* (1), 5-31.

Harré, R., & van Langenhove, L. (Eds.) (1999). *Positioning theory: Moral contexts of international action.* Oxford: Blackwell.

Hayward, K. (2008). The role of political discourse in conflict transformation: Evidence from Northern Ireland. *Peace and Conflict Studies, 15* (1), 1-20. Retrieved from https://nsuworks.nova.edu/cgi/viewcontent.cgi?article=1085&context=pcs.

Howarth, D., Norval, A. J., & Stavrakakis, Y. (Eds.) (1998). *Discourse theory and political analysis: Identities, hegemonies and social change.* Manchester: Manchester University Press.

Humanas Colombia–Centro Regional de Derechos Humanos y Justicia de Genero. (n.d.). Retrieved from https://humanas.org.co/alfa/index.php.

Lakoff, R. T. (1990). *Talking power.* New York: Basic Books.

Lakoff, R. T. (2000). *The language war.* Berkeley: University of California Press.

Mey, J. L. (2001). Pragmatics: An introduction (2nd ed.). Oxford: Blackwell Publishing.

Moghaddam, F., & Harré, R. (2010). Words, conflicts and political processes. In F. Moghaddam & R. Harré (Eds.), *Words of conflict, words of war: How the language we use in political processes sparks fighting* (pp. 1-30). Santa Barbara, CA: Praeger.

Olave, G. (2013). El proceso de paz en Colombia según el Estado y las Farc-ep. *Discurso & Sociedad,* 7 (2), 338-363.

Prieto-Mendoza, M. A. (2015, October). The meaning of the unsaid in the dialogues: Evidential analysis of the presuppositions in Colombia's Peace Dialogues. Paper presented at the 7th Dialogue Under Occupation (DUO VII) Conference, Porto Alegre, Brazil.

Romero-Trillo, J., & Maguire, L. (2011). Adaptative context: The fourth element of meaning. *International Review of Pragmatics, 3,* 228-241.

Sbisá, M. (2002). Speech acts in context. *Language & Communication, 22* (4), 421-436

Searle, J. R. (1969). *Speech acts.* Cambridge: Cambridge University Press.

Spradley, J. P. (1980). *Participant observation.* New York: Holt, Rinehart and Winston.

Valdeón García, R. (2009). Maurice: Translating the controversy, a comparative study of the English text and its Spanish version. *Meta: Journal des traducteurs/Meta: Translators' Journal, 54* (4), 704-732.

van Dijk, T. A. (1999). Critical discourse analysis and conversation analysis. *Discourse and Society, 10* (4), 459-460.

van Dijk, T. A. (2006). Ideology and discourse analysis. *Journal of Political Ideologies, 11* (2), 115-140.

Chapter 3

Oh, That's Just Crazy Talk:
How Leaders Use Language to Create
Perceptions of Irrationality

Jacob Ausderan[1]
Barry University, Miami Shores, Florida, United States

Abstract

In this chapter, I focus on the purposeful use of language by leaders around the world to create the perception that they are not rational actors (i.e., the use of language to make people think they're crazy). I take a qualitative approach and provide as many cases as will fit into the chapter of leaders (presidents, prime ministers, etc.) using language to create the perception that they are not rational actors. Leaders featured include John F. Kennedy from the United States of America, Richard Nixon from the United States of America, Idi Amin from Uganda, Francois Duvalier from Haiti, and both Kim Jong-il and Kim Jong-un from North Korea.

1. Introduction

NewsRadio was an American television sitcom airing from 1995-1999 that followed the trials and tribulations of a morning news station in New York City. Dave Nelson (played by Dave Foley) was the manager of the fictional WNYX radio station, while Matthew Brock (played by Andy Dick) was a news reporter at the same station and a frequent "thorn in the side" of the other characters, due to his annoying personality and habits.

One day, as Dave is talking to Matthew, Dave begins inserting random meows and barks in the middle of otherwise normal sentences, giving no indication that he is aware of what he is doing. For example: "Matthew! Get to the point–Meow!–okay?" Matthew is visibly confused and leaves Dave's office, telling him they can finish their conversation later. One of the other

---

[1] Assistant Professor, Department of History and Political Science, Barry University.

characters, having witnessed the strange back and forth, asks Dave what he is doing, to which Dave replies, "I have found from experience that sometimes the only way to get rid of Matthew is to act completely insane." The rest of the episode sees other characters emulating the tactic to varying degrees of success, sometimes with Matthew and sometimes with other characters who annoy them (*NewsRadio*, 1995).

Might this tactic prove useful for world leaders in their foreign policy dealings? If a leader makes a threat so outrageous that the threat, if carried out, would almost certainly lead to the leader's own destruction, or more generally, if the leader behaves in a manner that suggests he is irrational, then that leader's behavior becomes less predictable. This is because, in order to predict a person's behavior, some amount of rationality must be assumed (Bicchieri, 1987).[2] As Gross (1987) points out, "A large area of actions which can be anticipated as a ... decision of a rational state, escape normal expectation when an irrational state is involved" (p. 200). Similarly,

> a rational government cannot deal in the same way with an irrational one, with psychotic leaders ... Such policies are not effective, since irrational governments respond to different stimuli, its leaders perceive realities in a different way. [Ultimately,] policies have to be invented which could be effective toward such states. (p. 195)

Confronting potentially irrational leaders presents a unique foreign policy challenge that should be taken seriously by any government or foreign policy bureaucracy hoping to achieve success.

Although the previous chapter by Ibaños, Behle, and Penz (this volume) focuses on the rhetoric of private citizens in describing leaders (or candidates to become leader), this chapter focuses on the rhetoric of leaders themselves. As Berlin (this volume) points out, positioning is not only influenced by larger external factors, such as social and political contexts, but can be constructed by individuals through the use of discourse (Alcoff, 1988). A speaker engages in self-positioning–or first order positioning–when he promotes himself or his party or other self-interests through verbal means, sometimes purposefully and other times inadvertently (Harré & van Langenhove, 1999). I use this chapter to demonstrate that leaders from all over the world have acted "crazy" (whether purposefully or inadvertently) during foreign policy dealings, often achieving better outcomes in the process. I try to keep the focus on leaders'

---

[2] See Bicchieri (1987) for a description of the different types of rationality, including practical and epistemic.

rhetoric although I discuss decisions and actions when necessary, when exact quotes are not available for a particular incident.

2. Leadership and irrationality

Distinguishing between truly irrational behavior and behavior that has only the appearance of irrationality but is actually the result of a rational thought process presents challenges for any individual, group, or entity determining how to respond to that behavior. Indeed, it is important to distinguish between insanity and irrationality, since "[a] perfectly sane decision maker may act in an irrational way" (Gross, 1987, p. 197) while perceiving his action as being perfectly rational. In other words, sane people can act irrationally for some rational purpose, perhaps to ward off potential attacks from another country, or to gain a long-term advantage in negotiations, etc. Insane people, on the other hand, are not capable of distinguishing between rational and irrational behavior. By definition, they not capable of acting in their own best interests (i.e., rationally), although they may do so accidentally.

It is also possible for an individual's goals to be "insane" and for the actions taken to achieve those goals to be perfectly logical and rational. For example, while the murder of 6 million Jewish people, gypsies, etc. during the Holocaust may have been rational from the standpoint of achieving the Nazis' goals, and the actions taken by the Nazis in carrying out these murders were "efficient in terms of goal achievement," the goals themselves were "insane, cruel and escape a purely logical evaluation," simultaneously violating "our common sense judgement [and] elementary, moral imperatives of our civilization" and "irrational in terms of our culture and civilization" (Gross, 1987, p. 197).

Political philosophers, as far back as Niccolo Machiavelli, have argued that it can be "a very wise thing to simulate madness" (Machiavelli, 1996). More recently, Acharya and Grillo (2015) formalize the process by which leaders pretend to be crazy in order to achieve more favorable outcomes regarding international conflict. This model could be generalized and variance in the extent to which acting unpredictably is employed as a tactic, as well as the extent to which acting unpredictably proves successful in foreign policy crises, could be examined using a similar framework. Indeed, some scholars are already working along those lines (McManus, 2017).

The so-called Madman Theory is strongly associated with US President Richard Nixon. According to Nixon's Chief of Staff, H. R. Haldeman (1978), Nixon is said to have admitted, "I want the North Vietnamese to believe I've reached the point where I might do anything to stop the war. We'll just slip the word to them that, 'for God's sake, you know Nixon is obsessed about communism. We can't restrain him when he's angry–and he has his hand on the nuclear button' and Ho Chi Minh himself will be in Paris in two days begging for peace" (p. 122). Although this was not a public use of rhetoric, it was an instruction coming directly from Nixon to use specific words for a specific purpose; in this case, the words "obsessed" and "can't restrain him" imply that Nixon was an unstable actor.

On April 19, 1972, Nixon's National Security Advisor, Henry Kissinger, was preparing to fly to Moscow to meet with officials from the Soviet Union. Nixon's taping system recorded Kissinger giving Nixon the following advice: "The more reckless we appear [, the better] ... because after all, Mr. President, what we're trying to convince them of is that we are ready to go all the way" (Rosen and Nichter, 2014, ¶4). To which Nixon replied:

> Henry, we must not miss this chance, ... I'm going to destroy the goddamn country [North Vietnam], believe me, I mean destroy it, if necessary. And let me say, even [use] the nuclear weapon if necessary. It isn't necessary, but, you know, what I mean is, that shows you the extent to which I'm willing to go. (¶2)

Nixon's awareness of the taping system and his potential tampering with incriminating segments of tape during the Watergate scandal is well documented. Nixon knew that anything he said in the Oval Office could eventually become public, perhaps becoming known even to officials from the Soviet Union. His admission to Kissinger that he wanted to choose his words carefully–or that he wanted Kissinger to choose his own words carefully–in order to impress upon the Soviet Union the instability of Nixon's mental state, could have hindered Nixon's ability to use feigned irrationality to his advantage if the Soviet Union ever got ahold of the transcript of that conversation. If the Soviet Union overheard Nixon talking about the use of rhetoric to appear irrational, then they would know he wasn't truly irrational, and they would respond accordingly, with increased certainty regarding Nixon's mental state.

There are some indications, however, that Nixon occasionally forgot about his own taping system. While interviewing the man who actually set up the system, Alexander Butterfield, the interviewer asked whether Nixon ever "forgot about the fact that he was taping?" To which Butterfield replied:

> Absolutely. Yes. Yeah. We, we marveled at his ability to, uh, seemingly be oblivious to the tapes. I mean, even I was sitting there uncomfortably sometimes saying, 'He's not really going say this, is he?'

[laughter] But, but he did and I'm sure–[laughter] I'm sure John Dean can attest to that too.

As a follow-up, the interviewer asked: "Are you suggesting he was mechanically inept?" To which Butterfield replied: "Yeah, that was the suggestion [laughter]" (UVA Miller Center, 2017, ¶10-13).

3. John F. Kennedy and nuclear deterrence

Nixon may have learned something from one of his predecessors: John F. Kennedy. As soon as the United States and the Soviet Union had both developed nuclear weapons, it became the policy of both countries never to use nuclear weapons as offensive weapons, but as defensive weapons only. In other words, both countries agreed that they would never "strike first," but in retaliation only. This is where the concept of nuclear deterrence comes from: Having nuclear weapons for the purpose of scaring off other countries who might otherwise attack you. A state of mutually assured destruction is said to exist when two or more countries each have enough technology in place that they are able to retaliate with nuclear weapons even after suffering a first strike by the other country. The result is that neither country can attack the other without also causing their own destruction.

Because everyone seems to agree that it would be crazy to use nuclear weapons as a first-strike weapon, nuclear weapons aren't much of a threat as long as our leaders are rational. To some extent, this makes nuclear weapons a waste of money unless our leaders can show some potential for acting irrationally. Ultimately, a state of mutually assured destruction can only be created if one or more leaders believe that one or more of the other countries' leaders are crazy enough to actually use nuclear weapons as a first-strike weapon. The lengths to which some countries will go to create conditions in which mutually assured destruction is possible are sometimes comedic. Stanley Kubrick's film, *Dr. Strangelove*, was originally conceived as a dramatic thriller. However, while Kubrick was doing research on nuclear deterrence for his script, the sheer absurdity of mutually assured destruction and the lengths to which the two superpowers were willing to go during the Cold War convinced Kubrick that the movie should be a dark comedy. The Cuban Missile Crisis is simultaneously one of the most documented foreign policy crises in modern times and, until recently, when the CIA declassified a veritable treasure trove of documents relating to the crisis, one of the most mysterious. The crisis constituted a particularly strong challenge for a young president who had, during his presidential bid, essentially "red-baited" the opposing ticket, charging that the Eisenhower-Nixon administration had helped turn Cuba into "Communism's first Caribbean base." Indeed, because

Kennedy "had defined a tough stance toward Cuba as an important election issue, and given the humiliation he had suffered with the Bay of Pigs debacle, the missiles posed a great political hazard to Kennedy" (Schwarz, 2013). Some have even speculated that Kennedy strategically used language in his letters and public speeches to help give the impression that he was not entirely sane, in order to help in his negotiations with the Soviet Union over its nuclear missiles in Cuba, not unlike the fictitious Dave Nelson inserting meows into the middle of sentences on *NewsRadio*.

Although Kennedy had perfectly rational political motivations for turning the Soviet military presence in Cuba into the dominant issue of the 1960 presidential campaign, doing so may have accidentally led some European allies to determine that his fixation on the issue was insane. As Schwarz (2013) points out, Kennedy's extreme hostility toward Castro's regime led even Kennedy to admit that his attitudes were causing American allies in Europe to view him as "slightly demented."

At one point during the Cuban Missile Crisis, Kennedy faked a cold, using the media to leak the false information in order to fool the US public so that it didn't panic while Kennedy was hunkered down to deal with the crisis. According to the JFK Presidential Library, as soon as the Soviet missiles were identified on Cuba, the National Security Council (NSC) knew it had two policies to choose from: (a) an airstrike and/or invasion or (b) a quarantine of the entire island with potential further action depending on the circumstances. Moreover, "they needed to make a choice, but it had to happen in secret so the public didn't panic" (Eschner, 2017, ¶2). The President's staff quickly notified the press that Kennedy was suffering from a cold and would be returning to Washington, D.C. as soon as possible for some rest. The next day, while Kennedy was supposedly resting, he took the time for a vigorous pre-meeting swim and then met with the NSC to decide on a naval blockade of Cuba. Another day later, on October 22, Kennedy appeared on television and informed the public of his decision, making no mention of a cold and showing no apparent signs of illness. At that point, the deception became public knowledge (Eschner, 2017), not just to the American people, but also to allies and opponents abroad, perhaps influencing opinions on Kennedy's propensity for telling the truth and on Kennedy's capacity for sound judgment and decision-making.

A leader's threats often contain language and words meant specifically to create uncertainty regarding their intentions. For example, during a speech at the height of the Cuban Missile Crisis, President Kennedy remarked: "Let no one doubt that this is a difficult and dangerous effort on which we have set out. No one can foresee precisely what course it will take or what costs or casualties will be incurred" (The National Archives, n.d., ¶13). Marfleet (2000) argues that the uncertainty generated by Soviet actions and motives during the Cuban Missile Crisis caused Kennedy's beliefs to remain in a constant state of flux, and that Kennedy openly discussed his uncertainty regarding Soviet motives to Premier Khrushchev during private conversations.

Finally, it should be noted that Kennedy is said to have been worried about the sanity of some of his own advisors. Air Force General Thomas Power took an analyst from the Rand Corporation to task for suggesting that Russian cities should be spared from any potential nuclear first strike, saying: "Why are you so concerned with saving their lives? ... The whole idea is to *kill* the bastards ... At the end of the war, if there are two Americans and one Russian, we win" (Dallek, 2013, ¶10). This sort of talk worried Kennedy due to the freedom that some field commanders had to launch a nuclear strike without explicit permission from the President of the United States in the event of an imminent threat during which the President was not able to be contacted (or during which the President was *conveniently* not contacted).

4. Leaders outside the US

Idi Amin was President of Uganda from 1971-1979 and is notorious both for the brutality of his leadership and his erratic behavior. Although his insults of Europeans may have contributed to the media's portrayal of him as "unstable," it also caused Libya's Qaddafi to vigorously pursue an alliance with Uganda, and even led to friendly overtures from the Soviet Union. Meanwhile, debate raged within the European countries on the receiving end of Amin's insults over whether Amin was legitimately unhinged or merely using Europe as a scapegoat for political and economic upheaval in Uganda. Harold Wilson, the leader of the opposition party in Britain at the time, called Amin "mentally unbalanced" (Kaufman, 2003). Christopher Munnion, a journalist for a British newspaper called *The London Telegraph*, wrote the following: "Capricious, impulsive, violent and aggressive he certainly is, but to dismiss him as just plain crazy is to underestimate his shrewdness, his ruthless cunning and his capacity to consolidate power with calculated terror" (Kaufman, 2003, ¶12).

Turning to specific rhetoric from Amin during his tenure as president, although some of his comments during interviews and press conferences were truly bizarre–He once referred to cannibalism, saying, "It's not for me. I tried human flesh and it's too salty for my taste"–many of his comments demonstrate purposeful attempts to sow doubt about the extent to which his statements should be taken at face value. Amin is on record saying, "Sometimes people mistake the way I talk for what I am thinking" (*Daily Monitor*, 2015, ¶15) and that "If we knew the meaning to everything that is happening to us, then there would be no meaning" (¶3).

A retired CIA agent, John Mullen, who worked undercover in Uganda during the first two years of Amin's reign and even became Amin's basketball coach, said the following about Amin: "I wrote a book ... about [him] ... that is in stark contrast to what people in the agency have been saying about him. I didn't think Idi Amin was crazy. He was violent and ruthless, but I don't think what he did in Uganda was either mercurial or inexplicable" (Maxa, 1980, ¶2).

Turning to the Caribbean, Francois Duvalier–also known as "Papa Doc"–was a long-serving dictator of Haiti who knowingly took advantage of the public perception that he was somewhat crazy for political benefit. It should be noted that some of Duvalier's seemingly crazy behavior only appeared crazy to international audiences, and not to domestic audiences. Haiti has a very strong voodoo tradition. Duvalier kept himself on good terms with local voodoo priests and sorcerers, some of whom were feared by Haitians, and was even said to "indulge in voodoo rituals himself despite his scientific training and Roman Catholic background" (Krebs, 1971, p. 44). Several years before becoming President of Haiti, Duvalier wrote and published his own book on voodooism titled *Gradual Evolution of Voodoo*. As Duvalier accumulated support from lower-class Haitians using his embrace of voodooism, he also gained the support of the military, whose leadership considered him a malleable personality and a "useful idiot." Some of his campaign workers openly boasted that they could manipulate the man whom they served, some going as far as to make changes to Duvalier's speeches without his knowledge or permission.

Some Haitian intellectuals:

> who were later exiled have speculated that Duvalier, far from being a stupid pawn, cunningly stepped into a deceptive role as puppet and figurehead, playing various power blocs and interests against one another to divide and conquer. (Krebs, 1971, p. 44)

Whether Duvalier merely stumbled into power or was a mastermind who manipulated his way to the top, what is known is that once Duvalier became President of Haiti, hundreds of his political opponents were jailed. Some disappeared completely. According to one of Duvalier's top aides during this time, the president personally ordered more than 300 people killed during the first year alone (Krebs, 1971).

Although an argument can be made that Duvalier's embrace of voodooism and killing of political opponents were both rational behaviors (in the case of voodooism, perhaps even a necessary behavior in order to gain power), Duvalier did demonstrate some legitimately concerning behavior. When a top aide to Duvalier had to flee after an attempted coup, Duvalier's forces surrounded a house where the aide was thought to be hiding. When an old black dog came stumbling out of the house, Duvalier reacted to the superstitious belief that the aide in question could morph back and forth between human and black dog by ordering the killing of every black dog in the country (Krebs, 1971). Duvalier was later quoted as saying, "Bullets and machine guns capable of daunting Duvalier do not exist. They cannot touch me. I am already an immaterial being" (Abbott, 1988, p. 111).

Perhaps no regime in the modern era has been the subject of more debate over whether they are legitimately insane or merely "acting crazy" than the Kim regime in North Korea, particularly since the ascensions of Kim Jong-il in 1994 and Kim Jong-un in 2011.

As early as 1999, just 5 years into Kim Jong-il's reign, even members of the House International Relations Committee (who, it should be noted, have access to classified intelligence and should therefore know what they are talking about) were accusing US government policy of encouraging "all these crazy people over in North Korea to believe we are weaklings because we are giving them everything they want" (Cha & Kang, 2004, p. 231). On April 16th, 2017, US Senator John McCain, a member of the Senate Foreign Relations Committee and former Republican presidential nominee, had this exchange with Chuck Todd on NBC's *Meet the Press*:

> Sen. John McCain: … So this is really very serious. This guy in North Korea is not rational. His father and his grandfather were much more rational than he is.

> Chuck Todd: When you're dealing with an irrational actor, American presidents will always say with North Korea the military option is on the table but when you're dealing with an irrational actor as you just described does that make the military option actually something you don't want to deal with because you don't know how he's going to respond?

> Sen. John McCain: I think you never want to do that, again because of this proximity of North Korea artillery to Seoul, a city of how many million people. But at the same time to risk a situation where they have that ability and we rely on our ability to intercept, this could be the first test, the first real test of the Trump presidency … (NBC News, 2017, ¶59-61).

A legitimately crazy regime in East Asia, particularly one with nuclear weapons, would certainly make for good television ratings, and the US news media has been eager to latch onto the narrative and portray the regime as crazy. Newsweek published an issue in January 2003 with a picture of Kim Jong-il on the cover and the caption "Dr. Evil." Around the same time, Greta Van Susteren introduced a story on Fox News about Kim Jong-il by asking, "Is he insane or simply diabolical?" (Cha & Kang, 2004, p. 231).

On March 7, 2013, the North Korean Foreign Minister announced: "Now that the US is set to light a fuse for a nuclear war, the revolutionary armed forces of the DPRK will exercise the right to a preemptive nuclear attack to destroy the strongholds of the aggressors and to defend the supreme interests of the country" (Bennett, 2013, ¶3). Later that year, the North Korean government again threatened the United States, saying, "If you don't want to be a ghost in a hell fire, you better decide. We can give you only one suggestion. Run."[3] Although a direct strike upon United States territory would likely result in the total destruction of the ruling regime in North Korea, even threats that would be irrational if carried out can be made for rational reasons. Indeed, some scholars have already speculated that North Korean leader Kim Jong-un is purposefully pretending to be crazy in order to achieve a more favorable outcome (Simon, 2013).

Cha and Kang (2004) claims that

> The North undertakes limited but serious crisis-inducing acts of violence with the hope of leveraging crises more to its advantage, an extremely risky but also extremely rational policy for a country that has nothing to lose and nothing to negotiate with. (p. 232)

As discussed earlier, the peace generated by mutually assured destruction (MAD) only manifests when both sides believe that there is a greater-than-zero probability that the other side is willing to use nuclear weapons, even if doing so would lead to their own demise. In other words, the success of MAD depends on the creation of suspicion that the other side might be irrational, offering a ready-made explanation for the Kim regime's behavior as seemingly crazy, but perhaps crazy like a fox rather than legitimately insane.[4]

---

[3] Threat released by the North Korean government via propaganda pamphlets on December 16, 2013.

[4] Wagner (1991) formalizes the process by which countries convince potential adversaries that they will launch first strike counterforces with greater than zero probability. First strike counterforces are designed to wipe out an adversary's nuclear forces and eliminate their retaliatory capabilities.

5. Conclusion

I have used this chapter to demonstrate that leaders from all over the world have acted crazy–whether purposefully or inadvertently–and in the process engaged in self-positioning (Harré & van Langenhove, 1999). This is demonstrated by their use of language and rhetoric during their foreign policy dealings and speaks to a significant problem that governments and foreign policy bureaucracies sometimes face: given that world leaders often achieve better outcomes after demonstrating seemingly irrational behavior, how does one deal with such a leader when they don't know for sure whether they are truly irrational? In other words, how does one sort the crazies from the fakers?

It may never be possible to determine accurately and on a consistent basis whether a leader who demonstrates irrational behavior or who says things that suggest they are irrational is legitimately crazy or not. One possible solution is the use of textual analysis of a leader's words by companies, such as Social Science Automation.[5] Regardless, there are limits in the extent to which acting crazy in order to achieve better outcomes in foreign policy could be used successfully as a strategy. If a foreign leader repeatedly makes threats that would be irrational if carried out but never actually follows through, then, eventually, that leader's behavior becomes more predictable. Whereas the first threat may generate uncertainty (e.g., "Is he crazy? Is he sane? Will he follow through? We just don't know!"), repeated, similar threats that are never carried out cause that leader's behavior to become more predictable, therefore decreasing uncertainty regarding their behavior and making it more likely that threats that would be irrational if carried out are actually part of a rational decision-making process.

In the case of North Korea, it may become easier over time for the general public to see that Kim never had any intention of attacking the United States, but rather was aiming his remarks at a domestic audience. Although Kim Jong-un would cause his own destruction by carrying out his threat to preemptively attack the United States, he benefits on the domestic front from threatening to do so. The trick is to balance the risk of goading a foreign public with the domestic political benefit from making the threat. This is a balance that not all leaders are able to achieve. For example, although Saddam Hussein benefitted domestically by not cooperating fully with UN weapons inspections, he was unable to keep international public opinion from reaching the point where his country was invaded and he was deposed from power and eventually sentenced and killed.

---

[5] http://socialscience.net/.

Ultimately, politics is all about gaining and staying in power. For most leaders, this involves paying at least some attention to public opinion within the leader's country. The best option for confronting irrational behavior in other leaders may depend on how a leader's own public reacts to the foreign leader's supposedly irrational behavior. Ausderan (2018) shows that conservatives are more likely to support preemptive measures against foreign leaders who make irrational threats towards an individual's country (defined as a threat that would be irrational for the foreign leader to actually carry out) and that individuals with stronger dangerous world beliefs (i.e., a stronger disposition to view the world as inherently dangerous) are simultaneously more likely to view foreign leaders as irrational after hearing them make an irrational threat and less likely to attenuate their perceptions of irrationality after hearing the same leader make a more rational, follow-up threat.

Perhaps one solution to determining when and how to respond to world leaders who demonstrate behavior or use rhetoric that seems crazy is to take stock of the domestic public's reaction to the foreign leader's behavior. When is it more advisable for leaders or political candidates to make outrageous foreign policy threats? When are such threats more likely to be believed or responded to using force? The answers to these questions depend on the ideological makeup and societal worldviews of not only the threatening leader's own country, but also the target country. For example, a leader who wants to decrease domestic support for overseas military activity will find that telling their constituents that a foreign leader is perfectly rational is unlikely to decrease support for preemptive measures against that leader if their constituents are predisposed to view the world as dangerous. On the international stage, when attempting to repair one's image by making more rational and measured threats (imagine if Kim Jong-un announced that he was giving up nuclear weapons and then threatened some tamer, more strategic moves against the US in the South China Sea), such a move is less likely to reduce the probability of preemptive measures if the other country's general population has above average dangerous world beliefs (Ausderan, 2018).

Recall the example from the first paragraph of this chapter, when news station manager Dave Nelson randomly inserts meows and barks in the middle of otherwise normal sentences in order to get rid of a character named Matthew. The tactic is used by other characters for the remainder of the episode, sometimes against Matthew and sometimes against other characters, to mixed results. Indeed, the tactic does not work on everyone. But Dave Nelson knew that Matthew was predisposed to fall for the tactic and so he used it against him to great success. Not every employee is as lucky, but only because they employ the tactic against characters who do not share the same disposition.

References

Abbott, E. (1988). *Haiti: An insider's history of the rise and fall of the Duvaliers.* New York: Touchstone.

Acharya, A., & Grillo, E. (2015). War with crazy types. *Political Science Research and Methods, 3* (2), 281-307.

Alcoff, L. (1988). Cultural feminism versus post-structuralism: The identity crisis in feminist theory. *Signs, 13* (3), 405-436.

Ausderan, J. (2018). *Ideology, worldviews, and foreign policy attitudes towards irrational foreign leaders.* Manuscript in preparation.

Bennett, D. (2013, October 29). North Korea Is Now Threatening a Preemptive Nuclear Attack. *The Atlantic.* March 7, 2013. Retrieved on December 8, 2019, from https://www.theatlantic.com/international/archive/2013/03/north-korea-preemptive-nuclear-attack/317649/.

Berlin, L. N. (2020). The positioning of post-truth politics: Claims and evidence in the 2016 US presidential campaigns. In L. N. Berlin (Ed.), *Positioning and stance in political discourse: The individual, the party, and the party line*, (pp. 1-30). Wilmington, DE: Vernon Press.

Bicchieri, C. (1987). Rationality and predictability in economics. *The British Journal for the Philosophy of Science, 38* (4), 501-513.

Cha, V. D., & Kang, D. C. (2004). The debate over North Korea. *Political Science Quarterly, 119* (2), 229-254.

Daily Monitor. (2015, February 2). 10 Popular quotes by Idi Amin. Retrieved December 8, 2019, from https://www.monitor.co.ug/News/Insight/10-Popular-quotes-by-Idi-Amin/688338-2610284-m5xw3tz/index.html.

Dallek, R. (2018, April 17). JFK vs. the Military. Retrieved November 18, 2018, from https://www.theatlantic.com/magazine/archive/2013/08/jfk-vs-the-military/309496/.

Englebretson, R. (2007). Introduction. In R. Englebretson (Ed.), *Stancetaking in discourse: Subjectivity, evaluation, interaction* (pp. 1-26). Amsterdam/Philadelphia: John Benjamins.

Eschner, K. (2017, October 20). JFK Faked a Cold to Get Back to Washington During the Cuban Missile Crisis. Retrieved September 30, 2018, from https://www.smithsonianmag.com/smart-news/jfk-faked-cold-get-back-washington-during-cuban-missile-crisis-180965308/.

Gross, F. (1987). Reflexions on a rational state and Europe. *Il Politico, 52* (2), 193-211.

Haldeman, H. R. (1978). *The ends of power.* New York: Times Books.

Harré, R., & van Langenhove, L. (1999). *Positioning theory: Moral contexts of intentional action.* Oxford: Blackwell Publishers Ltd.

John F. Kennedy Library. (2003). Alexander Butterfield Explains the Nixon Taping System: Miller Center. Retrieved November 4, 2018, from https://millercenter.org/alexander-butterfield-explains-nixon-taping-system.

Kaufman, M. T. (2003, August 17). Idi Amin, murderous and erratic ruler of Uganda in the 70's, dies in exile. New York Times. Retrieved from https://www.nytimes.com/2003/08/17/world/idi-amin-murderous-and-erratic-ruler-of-uganda-in-the-70-s-dies-in-exile.html.

Krebs, A. (1971, April 23). Papa Doc, a ruthless dictator, kept the Haitians in illiteracy and dire poverty. New York Times. Retrieved from https://www.nytimes.com/1971/04/23/archives/papa-doc-a-ruthless-dictator-kept-the-haitians-in-illiteracy-and.html.

Machiavelli, N. (1996). *Discourses on Livy* (H. C. Mansfield & N. Tarcov, Trans.). Chicago: University of Chicago Press. (Original work published c. 1517).

Marfleet, B. G. (2000). The operational code of John F. Kennedy during the Cuban Missile Crisis: A comparison of public and private rhetoric. *Political Psychology, 21* (3), 545-558.

Maxa, R. (1980, January 6). Our CIA man in Idi Amin's Uganda. *The Washington Post.* Retrieved from https://www.washingtonpost.com/archive/lifestyle/magazine/1980/01/06/our-cia-man-in-idi-amins-uganda/264b533a-c029-46fe-8e66-a2e44f9d7a80/.

McManus, R. W. (2017). *Crazy like a fox? Do leaders perceived as mentally unstable achieve better conflict outcomes?* Manuscript in preparation.

Mele, A. R. (1987). *Irrationality: An essay on akrasia, self-deception, and self-control.* New York: Oxford University Press.

NBC News. (2017, April 16). Meet the Press–April 16, 2017. Retrieved December 8, 2019, from https://www.nbcnews.com/meet-the-press/meet-press-april-16-2017-n747116.

NewsRadio. 1995. Episode "4:20," Season 4, Episode 20. Retrieved December 8, 2019, from https://www.springfieldspringfield.co.uk/view_episode_scripts.php?tv-show=newsradio-1995&episode=s04e20.

Rosen, J., & Nichter, L. A. (2014, March 25). Madman in the White House. Retrieved October 7, 2018, from https://foreignpolicy.com/2014/03/25/madman-in-the-white-house/.

Schwarz, B. (2013, February). The real Cuban Missile Crisis. Retrieved September 30, 2018, from https://www.theatlantic.com/magazine/archive/2013/01/the-real-cuban-missile-crisis/309190/.

Simon, H. (2013). Kim Jong-un and the "Madman Theory" of diplomacy. Retrieved from https://origins.osu.edu/history-news/kim-jong-un-and-madman-theory-diplomacy.

The National Archives. (n.d.). Education | Heroes & Villains | John Kennedy | Source 1 | Transcript. Retrieved December 8, 2019, from https://nationalarchives.gov.uk/education/heroesvillains/transcript/g2cs2s1t.htm.

UVA Miller Center. (2017, March 17). Alexander Butterfield Explains the Nixon Taping System. Retrieved from https://millercenter.org/alexander-butterfield-explains-nixon-taping-system.

Wagner, R. H. (1991). Nuclear deterrence, counterforce strategies, and the incentive to strike first. *American Political Science Review, 85* (3), 727-749.

Chapter 4

Trump vs. Clinton:
Implicatures as Public Stance Acts

Chi-Hé Elder
University of East Anglia, Norwich, United Kingdom

Abstract

This chapter contributes to the study of stance in political discourse by demonstrating how implicatures–as implicit aspects of meaning inferable from a given utterance–can be publicly targeted as the object of a stance act to promote one's own political stance. Focusing on the institutional context of political debate, it identifies different ways in which the 2016 US presidential candidates, Donald Trump and Hillary Clinton, used and manipulated implicatures to affiliate or disaffiliate themselves with the stance of their opponent, in turn promoting their own stance as legitimate. By adding implicatures to our arsenal of explanatory tools for the study of stance, this chapter provides a new insight into the interactional role that implicatures play as a discursive tool, demonstrating how the multiplicity of meanings that are implicit yet inferable from a single utterance can be used in communicatively deviant ways to discredit the views of another, while drawing attention to and supporting one's own personal and political motives.

1. Introduction

The act of taking a stance involves two crucial ingredients: (a) the stance that a speaker takes through their stance act, and (b) the object to which the speaker takes a stance. With respect to (a), there are many types of stance that one can take, including (but certainly not limited to) epistemic stance (e.g., Clift, 2006; Heritage & Raymond, 2005; Kärkkäinen, 2003; Martín de la Rosa, Domínguez Romero, Pérez Blanco, & Marín-Arrese, this volume), affective stance (e.g., Haviland, 1991; Ochs, 1996), and interpersonal stance (e.g., Kiesling, 2009). But while many studies have identified stance markers as overt linguistic expressions of different types of stance (e.g., "I know" is said to express positive epistemic stance, while "that's great" expresses positive affective stance), it is well known that the different types of stance are not mutually exclusive: a single utterance can be used to express different types of stance at the same time. So, rather than viewing stance as a semantic notion that is observable from explicit linguistic markers, stance is better seen as a pragmatic notion: an interactive activity that occurs between conversational participants.

Since DuBois' (2007) introduction of the "stance triangle," it is now well acknowledged that the act of taking a stance not only positions a speaker with respect to a previous utterance (i.e., ingredient (b) above, the stance object), but it also involves aligning (or disaligning) the speaker with respect to other interlocutors. Alignment can be done linguistically (e.g., by saying "I agree" to signal agreement), non-linguistically by a nod of the head, or even implicitly by simply responding appropriately to the prior turn (cf. Walker, 1996). In fact, the object of stance itself is also something that is pragmatically, as opposed to semantically, realized, as often a prior utterance to which a speaker is taking a stance includes implicitly recoverable elements, thus requiring the uttered sentence to be "filled in" with information from the extralinguistic context. A simple example of this is the recovery of referents for inherently contextual indexicals, such as the referent for "that" in "that's great." Combining these two ingredients (a) and (b) together, it becomes clear that stancetaking is a complex, multidimensional interactional move that involves linguistic, non-linguistic, and extralinguistic information for its interpretation.

This chapter takes further the idea that the act of taking a stance involves implicit communication in two respects. First, it takes seriously the idea that the act of taking a stance need not be linguistically observable: while agreement can be signaled implicitly, this chapter advances the view that stancetaking can be achieved via implicitly communicated implicatures (Grice, 1975). Second, this chapter promotes the importance of examining the "stance follow" (DuBois, 2007) in interpreting stance. On the one hand, an interlocutor's response to a previous stance act–the stance follow–constitutes a further stance act in and of itself. But as I discuss, the stance follow plays an equally important role of making public how the initial speaker's stance act has been "operationalized" (Arundale, 2013) in the current interaction, whether it was intended to be as such by the initial speaker. So overall, this chapter demonstrates that a stance act can target an implicitly communicated implicature available in a prior turn, whether intentionally communicated or not, indicating that the object of stance need not always be found in explicit linguistic utterances.

The data under discussion are the 2016 US presidential debates between Donald Trump and Hillary Clinton (cf. Berlin, this volume). Political discourse is an apt source for the study of implicit meanings, as non-literal implicatures can be used by politicians to their advantage as they can communicate messages without being explicit; yet, as the messages are off-record, they can retain plausible deniability of those effects. Furthermore, politicians can exploit the use of non-literal language in interaction by attending to an opponent's explicit or implicit content, regardless of whether it was intended, to signal their disaffiliation with the stance of their opponent (e.g., Nuolijarvi & Tiittula, 2011). Indeed, by challenging the stance of an opponent, an interlocutor can hold the other accountable to a stance whose fact is in dispute (Keisanen, 2007). Through the lens of interactional pragmatics (e.g., Elder & Haugh, 2018), in this chapter I examine how Donald Trump and Hillary Clinton used and manipulated implicatures to affiliate or disaffiliate themselves with the stance of their opponent, in turn promoting their own stance as legitimate. Note that in this chapter I remain politically neutral, making no claims as to which candidate was more deceptive than the other.

The structure of this chapter is as follows. In Section 2, I demonstrate how the concepts of stance and implicature, despite stemming from different theoretical traditions, can be usefully combined for the purpose of empirical data analysis, allowing implicitly communicated implicatures to constitute the object of a stance act as well as to communicate stance itself. In Section 3, I move to consider the role of implicatures in the specific context of political discourse, identifying interactional resources that political actors can utilize to garner audience support, even in the relative absence of direct interpersonal interaction. Section 4 presents an analysis of three critical extracts from the 2016 US presidential debates, exemplifying some key discursive strategies that Clinton and Trump employed for the expression of stance, focusing on how they negotiated and manipulated implicatures of the other for their own purposes. Finally, Section 5 brings together the key findings of the chapter, commenting on how the studies of stance and implicature can productively and usefully inform one another.

2. Implicatures as indirect stance markers

Stance is given a heterogeneous treatment in the extant literature, both in terms of definition and of approach, spanning work in variationist sociolinguistics, anthropological linguistics, and, of relevance here, in interactional pragmatics (see Jaffe, 2009, for an overview). Following DuBois (2007), I take stance to be the public act of positioning oneself with respect to the content of what is said, and/or with respect to one's interlocutors.

As a public act, an obvious question concerns how people communicate stance via observable features of discourse. One way to address this question is to examine words and phrases that typically function as stance markers. In their seminal paper, Biber and Finegan (1988) looked at the use of adverbials (e.g., "honestly," "generally," "actually") as epistemic stance markers, being "the overt expression of an author's or speaker's attitudes, feelings, judgments, or commitment concerning the message" (Biber & Finegan, 1988, p. 1). However, despite such attempts, it transpires that identifying stance markers is not a straightforward task for the two reasons that (a) there are many different types of stance, and (b) pinpointing types from a given stance act–if this is a desirable endeavor at all–is not an easily achievable task.

Here is a brief survey of options of the types of stance that one can express. First, epistemic stance is said to reflect the degree of certainty that a speaker has towards the content of what is said, typically indicated through stance markers such as "I think" or "I know." Epistemic stance is then contrasted with other kinds of stance. On the one hand, while epistemic stance concerns certainty towards what is said, affective (or evaluative) stance is concerned with the speaker's attitude towards a given target (for example through evaluative phrases, such as "that's horrible" or "that's wonderful," cf. Field, 1997; Ochs, 1996). A slightly different distinction is offered by Kiesling (2009), who differentiates epistemic stance from interpersonal stance, the latter being a person's expression of their relationship with others, ranging from friendly to dominating. He emphasizes that epistemic and interpersonal stance are inherently interrelated, as a person's certainty in their assertion can be simultaneously linked to their attitude towards the other person and the status of their knowledge. Finally, rather than separating the different kinds of stance, other scholars include aspects of interpersonal relationships in the concept of epistemic stance itself, so that epistemic stance encompasses not only a speaker's certainty in their assertions, but also whether the speaker agrees with what others say, or whether the speaker views themselves as more or less knowledgeable than their interlocutors (e.g., Ochs & Schieffelin, 1989).

Given the proliferation of different types of stance that a single stance act can express, DuBois (2007) has motivated analyzing acts of stancetaking from a dialogic point of view. How people assess the stance of their interlocutors is not only down to the words that they utter, but the interaction of their utterances with other "socially salient" aspects of the speaker: other utterances the speaker has previously made; their manner of speaking (voice quality, accent, pitch); information about the speaker's identity and life, and so forth; the object of stance; and crucially, the stance to which the stancetaker is responding: the proposition that is being aligned or disaligned with.

Together, these components are brought together in what DuBois terms the "stance triangle": interlocutors use their utterances to position themselves not only with respect to the object of stance, but also with respect to other interlocutors. As he says, since "participants routinely monitor who is responsible ... for any given stance, the very act of taking a stance becomes fair game to serve as a target for the next speaker's stance" (DuBois, 2007, p. 141). He exemplifies this claim through a number of examples serving to show that the object of a stance act is often implicitly marked by the speaker, to be located in the prior discourse. Even when a speaker uses an explicit stance marker, for example, an affective marker such as "I'm glad," or an epistemic marker such as "I know," the object of that stance (i.e., the object about which the speaker is glad or that the speaker knows) requires filling in by the prior discourse, rendering the expression of stance as at least partially implicitly communicated.

The idea that stance, as a public act, can be expressed implicitly provides the first hint that the search for overt stance markers cannot tell us the whole story *vis-à-vis* the expression of stance. Instead, viewing stance as something that is interactionally achieved (cf. Sacks et al., 1974; Schegloff, 1981) moves us away from the assumption that types of stance can be expressed by specific linguistic forms, even when those linguistic forms are subject to contextual calibration in view of their being expressed in a particular context of utterance.

Thus, despite stemming from different theoretical traditions, we can see clear links between the concept of stance, as intersubjective and context-dependent, with contextualist, interactionist views on propositional meaning. Here I take the dialogic study of stance a step further by drawing attention to the fact that it is not only that the object of stance may be implicit insofar as referents of context-dependent indexicals need to be recovered (which can be difficult to pin down precisely), but that the object of stance may not have been explicitly expressed in the first place.

Drawing insight from philosophical pragmatics, we know that a speaker can communicate messages indirectly via implicitly communicated implicatures (Grice, 1975). Implicatures are typically theorized as aspects of meaning that the speaker intends to communicate to the hearer, and hence that the speaker intends the hearer to recover. To explain how hearers are able to smoothly recover the meanings of such implicatures, Grice proposed conversational maxims that interlocutors are expected to adhere to in communication, from which hearers are able to work out what a speaker meant by a given utterance. However, Grice (1975, pp. 39-40) also admitted that an utterance can simultaneously communicate a possibly open-ended list of implicatures, making it difficult to pinpoint exactly what the intended meaning was. So rather than theorizing implicatures as speaker intended aspects of meaning, when we acknowledge the multiplicity of potential inferences from a single utterance, we can instead view implicatures as lying on a cline from strong to weak: from those that are clearly inferable, determinate in content, and expected to have been intended by the speaker, to those that are weakly communicated, either because the meaning is indeterminate, or because it was unlikely to have been intended by the speaker (cf. Elder, 2019). At the extreme end of the cline are those aspects of meaning that lie outside the remit of what the speaker could have plausibly intended, yet could arguably be recovered by the hearer on account of the speaker having normative responsibility for the things that they say. As far as the object of stance is concerned, it is any of these implicatures–whether strongly or weakly communicated–that a speaker makes available via their utterances that can constitute fair game for another interlocutor to draw on in the following turn.

Admittedly, allowing stance to be implicitly expressed presents a challenge for empirical observations of stance. However, just because stance can be expressed implicitly does not render taking a stance as no longer a public act. Elder and Haugh (2018) have recently proposed a model of the process of negotiating propositional meanings as non-summative interactional achievements through on-record linguistic action, showing how interlocutors can draw on inferable aspects of their communicative partners, even when those aspects of meaning were not intended to be communicated. That is, by responding to an utterance in a particular way, a speaker not only makes publicly available an inference about what they themselves mean by their own utterance, but they also make publicly available an inference about how they have understood the utterance to which they are responding. In turn, when a speaker makes a public act of responding to an utterance of a previous speaker, that previous speaker is held accountable for the meaning they have communicated in virtue of it having been made the object of a future utterance (cf. Berlin, this volume).

The view that a speaker's response to a previous utterance can determine how the previous utterance has been operationalized is directly analogous to DuBois' (2007) emphasis on the importance of looking at the "stance follow"– the audience or interlocutor uptake of a stance act in the form of their own stance act–in determining the initial stance. That is, by targeting an implicitly expressed stance from the content of a previous speaker's utterance, the object of the following stance act is made public as it constitutes an inferable aspect of the initial speaker's utterance, even if that speaker did not intend to communicate it. So, implicatures, despite being implicitly communicated, in their sequential context are no less inferable than the meanings of explicit linguistic markers, and hence remain to be considered public.

Here I extend the scope of application of Elder and Haugh's (2018) model to demonstrate how implicatures can be targeted as the object of stance. However, while the aim of their model as it stands is to track the meanings that are mutually and manifestly co-constructed between interlocutors, it has to be acknowledged that interlocutors do not always enter discursive situations with the aim of achieving mutual agreement on meanings. As Grice (1989) himself noted, "collaboration in achieving exchange of information or the institution of decisions may coexist with a high degree of reserve, hostility, and chicanery" (p. 369). Political debate is thus an apt context for exemplification, given that it is typically constructed with the aim of promoting one's own political agenda, and that divergent communicative aims between interlocutors are common. Moreover, the language of political debate is inherently manipulative, insofar as it aims to push certain political ideologies with the purpose of obtaining support from relevant audiences (Berlin, this volume).

In the following sections, I examine how individual speakers make particular meanings salient–either of their own utterances or of another's– using the institutional format of political debate as a test site. Specifically, I look at both how implicitly expressed implicatures can be used by a speaker to legitimize their own stance (or delegitimize another's stance), as well as how speakers exploit unintended, yet nevertheless available inferences of another speaker to pit one speaker's stance against the other's. In this respect, I capitalize on DuBois' (2007) hint that "[t]he role of implicit stance alignment will prove to be especially important in the management of intersubjectivity" (p. 144), demonstrating how the act of taking a stance can be publicly achieved through the use, negotiation, and manipulation of implicitly communicated implicatures.

3. Implicature as an interactional resource in political debate

Drawing on Hall's (1976) distinction between high-context and low-context communication, Heylighen and Dewaele (2002) distinguish high-context situations from low-context situations, where the former pertain to informal situations in which individual utterances are subject to a high degree of contextual interpretation, while the latter pertain to more formal settings where ambiguities are easily disambiguated by explicit information. Political debates, typically adhering to a fixed turn structure led by a moderator, and with both a live and televised audience, would typically be categorized as low-context situations. As such, it is expected that messages should be unambiguously constructed, with minimal use of nonliteral, context-dependent language in order to avoid misunderstandings. This is in contrast to more interactive settings in which multiple interlocutors may be expected to use highly contextual language.

However, despite its formal nature, political discourse is built using many contextual cues and indexical meanings as the political actors aim to obtain support from the audience by appealing to emotion, subjectivity and commonalities (Berlin, this volume; Reyes, 2015). Previous studies have examined various interactional resources that are used in political discourse, even when one-on-one interaction is rare. In the case of political speeches, Reyes (2015) notes how the use of pronouns such as "you" and "we"–which are inherently contextual–can be used to position a political actor with respect to their audience, thereby building rapport and intimacy (Prieto-Mendoza, this volume), while audiences can contribute to the collaborative construction of a politician's meaning through their laughter and applause (cf. Berlin, 2012). Similarly, Kampf (2016) observes how "speech acts of solidarity" (e.g., congratulating, greeting, and blessing) can be used by politicians to a strategic end to display their (dis)affiliations with others.

Although communicative interaction between participants is much more limited than in everyday interaction, political debates do have more scope for two-way communication than in political speeches. As such, we can expect participants to draw on a wider range of interactional resources in order to target previous utterances in the discourse as the object of stance. One such interactional resource is the interrogative. Koshik (2003) observes how wh-interrogatives can be used in contexts of already established disagreement and thus, in those cases, do not function as requests for responses. Rather, they are treated as challenges of previous utterances, expressing negative epistemic stance towards a previous claim. Keisanen (2007) takes these observations further, looking at how negative yes/no interrogatives ("don't you mean...?"), negative assertions followed by a positive tag question ("...have you?"), and positive assertions followed by a negative tag question ("... isn't it?"), can all do the work of challenging prior stances. The challenge is constructed by displaying doubt towards a claim or stance embedded in a previous turn, both suggesting that the stance is somehow problematic while also holding the recipient (i.e., the author of the claim) accountable for it. As Keisanen (2007) says, "[b]y singling out some (explicitly or implicitly expressed) claim or position in the prior turn, discourse participants can call the interactional positioning implicated in the voicing of such claims or positions into question. On occasion, then, taking a stance can be treated as an accountable action" (pp. 277-278).

These studies on the use of interrogatives thus show how a prior turn can be targeted as the object of stance. We can project the applicability of these findings more widely by also hypothesizing that the object of stance need not be explicitly uttered, but may be implicitly assumed as common ground with another participant, or may be available as an implicature derivable from the propositional content of a previous utterance. But furthermore, the use of an interrogative as a challenging device, as opposed to a request for information, is a way of communicating stance indirectly. That is, the challenging interrogatives themselves communicate an implicature of a negative assertion, indicating the speaker's disagreement with the truth, or even existence, of a prior claim.

In the same way that certain specific structural constructions can be used for the purpose of simultaneously communicating multiple messages, Nuolijarvi and Tiittula (2011) look at how the use of irony is exploited in political debate as a source of ambiguity in order to criticize opponents. On the one hand, ironic utterances can be used mockingly in order to display disaffiliation with another's stance. But, as they demonstrate, the inherent ambiguous nature of irony also means that it can be interactionally exploited by the recipient by ignoring the unforgiving non-literal interpretation, and instead treating the ironic turn at face value in order to highlight its inappropriateness. On the other hand, it is exactly because ironic turns convey more than one proposition (i.e., different explicit and implicit meanings) that conversational participants can draw on one or other meanings for their own purposes, whether that is by ignoring clearly intended aspects of meaning of another speaker that do not fit with their own desired communicative direction, or by exploiting unintended aspects of meaning to ridicule the other's stance.

Here I broaden the scope of inquiry beyond the specific case of irony, looking more generally at the role of implicatures in the negotiation and manipulation of meanings in political debate. As I have already hinted, given the fixed turn, formal nature of the debates, implicit messages would be expected to be minimal. This is because, in everyday communication, implicatures typically rely on contextual information for their recovery which can require recourse to shared knowledge between the interlocutors that is not recoverable to outside participants. However, given the purpose of political debate is not simply to exchange information between the participants themselves, but to appeal to both live and televised audiences for their political support, the success of implicitly communicated messages rests on the speakers constructing their utterances in such a way so as to be inferable by a third-party audience who lack the shared knowledge of the two interlocutors.

In this sense, we might expect political actors to engage in more effortful, cognitively-loaded communicative strategies, exactly because of the high degree of intentionality that goes into the preparation of such high-stakes interactions. As Bond, Homan, Eggert, Speller, Garcia, Majia, McInnes, Ceniceros, and Rustige (2017) state in a study of language processing in political debate, "when [political actors] plan false intentions in order to deceive the electorate or other candidates to paint a rosy future, or when they engage in twisting facts, they do so within a high-stakes political sociocultural context, which taxes cognitive capacity because these deceptive strategies are, arguably, highly effortful" (p. 675). In other words, it is arguably due to the high stakes, formal nature of the debate, that we can expect the candidates to draw on implicatures as a useful interactional resource in the promoting of their own political agenda, both as the target of an aligning or disaligning stance act, or as an implicit yet inferable stance act in and of itself.

4. Manipulating implicatures in the 2016 US Presidential Debates[1]

The US presidential debates of 2016 between Donald Trump and Hillary Clinton broke the record for the highest number of viewers in the history of televised presidential debates (Katz, 2016). While in political discourse it is typical to see politicians loading their utterances with truth and authority to increase their legitimization and hence promoting their stance towards established facts (cf. Chilton, 2004), at the height of the so-called "post-truth era" (Berlin, this volume), the 2016 presidential debates saw several instances of the candidates not only arguing over the facts thereby discrediting one candidate's stance towards accepted facts against the other, but also calling into question the other's stance over the facts themselves. But arguably one of the reasons the debates were so widely watched was that the debates involved not only disputes over political opinions and proposed policies, but also personal attacks that called into question the other candidate's fitness for office. While leadership debates typically serve the purpose of candidates garnering audience support by demonstrating authority and command of the topics at hand, the 2016 presidential debates saw the two candidates frequently taking a stance on issues relating to the other's unfavorable personal attributes to persuade voters. During the campaign, Donald Trump infamously branded his competitor "Crooked Hillary" following the charges against her for using a personal email server for official communications (e.g., Schallhorn, 2018), while Hillary Clinton criticized Trump's tweeting behavior, describing him as "temperamentally unfit" for the presidency, even posing a threat to national security (Luscombe, 2016; cf. Ausderan, this volume; Ibaños, Behle, & Penz, this volume).

In this section, I look at some of the ways that Trump and Clinton drew on different meanings inferable from the other's previous turn in order to promote their own stance, not only towards accepted (or indeed, contested) "facts," but also towards the personal attributes of their opponent.

---

[1] All transcripts for this chapter have been adapted for presentational purposes from those obtained from the website http://politicaladarchive.org/debate-project/ (Internet Archive, 2016).

Specifically, I start by looking at (a) how they capitalized on negatively construed explicit meanings, before moving to (b) how they ignored strong, clearly inferable implicatures of their opponent, and finally, (c) how they exploited strong, clearly inferable implicatures of their opponent.

4.1. Disaffiliation of stance by capitalizing on negatively construed explicit meanings

In the lead up to extract (1), the topic of the debate is taxation. During the course of the discussion, two controversial issues are raised, namely of Trump not releasing his tax return, and of Clinton using a private email server for official communications.

(1)

1 TRUMP	We have a country that needs new roads, new tunnels, new bridges, new airports, new schools, new hospitals
2	And we don't have the money, because it's been squandered on so many of your ideas
3 HOLT	We'll let you respond and we'll move on to the next segment
4 CLINTON	And maybe because you haven't paid any federal income tax for a lot of years
	[AUDIENCE APPLAUSE]
5	And the other thing I think is important–
6 TRUMP	It would be squandered too, believe me

In this extract, we see both Trump and Clinton drawing on the explicit content of the other, reframing negative charges against themselves as negative charges against the other. First, in line 1, Trump outlines a number of public facilities that require funding, before in line 2 stating that "we don't have the money" because Clinton "squandered" public funds on her "ideas."[2] Despite Trump charging Clinton with the blame for the national debt, Clinton

---

[2] Earlier in the debate, Trump accuses Clinton of supporting Bill Clinton in the NAFTA agreement, which Trump describes as "the single worst trade deal ever approved in this country." Trump also accuses Clinton of supporting the Trans-Pacific Partnership, which he claims she had previously referred to as "the gold standard." According to the Internet Archive (2016), the "Gold Standard" clip was the third most broadcast clip by the major cable news channels and morning news programs in the 26 hours following the debate.

prefaces her own explanation for the lack of spending money in line 4 with the conjunction "and," thus presenting an additional explanation to Trump's as opposed to an alternative one. In this way, she implicitly, even if unintentionally, aligns herself with Trump's just prior claim, endorsing his statement of blame against her.

Nevertheless, Clinton's new explanation for the lack of available spending money, namely that Trump hasn't "paid any federal income tax for a lot of years," draws attention away from her past wrongdoings, making explicit a charge against Trump that hitherto has only been made speculatively on the basis of his not having released his tax return. In line 6, Trump responds to Clinton's allegation by employing exactly the same discursive strategy that Clinton did in line 4. That is, he does not dispute Clinton's claim, and so implicitly aligns himself with its content (again, whether or not intentionally). In fact, by posing the counterfactual "it would be squandered too," Trump implicitly communicates the elided condition "if he had paid his federal tax," which in turn communicates the presupposition that the condition is false: in other words, it presupposes that he has not paid his federal tax, thereby strengthening his alignment with Clinton's claim. However, this alignment may only be a byproduct of the overarching aim of the utterance, namely as it serves to draw attention back to Clinton's previously alleged spending, emphasizing that even if he had paid his federal tax, it would not be available to spend now, because Clinton would have spent it, further communicating the negative charge that with the availability of any funds, Clinton would have ill-advisedly spent them.

What we see in this extract is both Trump and Clinton communicating negative evaluative stance towards the actions of the other through their explicit jibes, presenting on record allegations against the other for the reason behind the national debt. In response, Clinton and Trump both utilize the same discursive strategy of elaborating on the explicit content of what has just been said, at the same time drawing attention away from their own past wrongdoings and towards negative charges against the other. However, in not explicitly disputing the just prior claim of their opponent, they both, possibly inadvertently, align themselves with the content of the other's allegations. Nevertheless, Trump's use of the counterfactual conditional is arguably more successful as a discursive strategy than Clinton's use of the conjunction, as the conditional serves to highlight that the charge against Trump is irrelevant in light of the charge against Clinton.

4.2. Disaffiliation of stance by ignoring strong implicatures

In extract (2), we see Trump and Clinton pursuing analogous discursive strategies to those in the previous extract, except that in the following case, they target implicitly communicated meanings as opposed to explicit meanings. In the discussion leading up to the following extract, the topic is on creating jobs. Trump criticizes Clinton's proposal, in which she makes reference to her website where viewers can "fact check" Trump's claims and view her own proposal. As they come to the end of the segment on creating jobs, Trump refers back to Clinton's website, shifting the topic as follows.

(2)

1 TRUMP	And look at her website. You know what? It's no different than this. She's telling us how to fight ISIS. Just go to her website. She tells you how to fight ISIS on her website	
2	I don't think General Douglas MacArthur would like that too much	
3 HOLT	The next segment, we're continuing –	
4 CLINTON	Well, at least I have a plan to fight ISIS	
5 HOLT	– achieving prosperity –	
6 TRUMP	No, no, you're telling the enemy everything you want to do	
7 CLINTON	No, we're not. No, we're not	

In line 1 of this extract, Trump makes reference to Clinton's plan to fight ISIS being available on her website, following up with a jibe in line 2, "I don't think General Douglas MacArthur would like that too much." This remark carries three strongly inferable aspects of meaning. First, it communicates the explicit content regarding the projected opinion of General Douglas MacArthur. Second, it carries the strongly inferable implicature that publishing her plan online is not a good strategy, thereby publicly disaligning Trump from Clinton's ISIS strategy. However, the recoverability of this strong implicature does not mean that the explicit content does not do further work as, third, the indexical "that" refers back to the content explicitly available in the previous turn, thus also entailing the assertion "she tells you how to fight ISIS on her website." All three of these meanings communicate negative evaluative stance towards Clinton's ISIS strategy.

In line 4, Clinton interrupts the moderator to respond to Trump. While we might expect her to draw on any of his three meanings available from line 2 and to refute his claims, this is not what happens. Admittedly, her use of "at least" serves in part to minimize the strength of Trump's previous allegation, thereby displaying reduced epistemic stance towards his claims. However, she does not outright refute them; instead, by stating "at least I have a plan," she implicitly supports both Trump's assertion that her ISIS plan is on her website, and, moreover, his implicature that her plan being online is not a good idea. In this way, she actually aligns herself with those two claims. This may seem like a surprising rhetorical strategy. However, what we do see is Clinton countering Trump's available meanings in the prior turn with her own verbal attack. That is, by stating, "at least I have a plan to fight ISIS," she puts focus on "I," thereby communicating her own strong implicature, namely that the other salient political actor–i.e., Trump–does not have a plan to fight ISIS. So, rather than responding to Trump's negative charges, she turns attention away from the topic of her strategy being questionable, towards the positive claim that it is better to have a plan than not.

In line 6, Trump responds to Clinton's remark (again, interrupting the moderator). However, he does not acknowledge her clearly inferable implicature condemning his lack of plan, and instead responds to the explicit content of her utterance disputing her assertion "I have a plan." However, just because Trump did not acknowledge the implicature, does not mean that he did not recognize it. As Drew (1987) notes with regard to teasing, "[a]lthough the only research methodology for seeing that someone has recognized a tease is through their displaying that recognizing (for example, by laughing) it cannot be inferred from an absence of such a display that they did not recognize the tease" (p. 226). That is, the lack of displaying recognition towards Clinton's implicature does not entail that there was no recognition tout court.

Instead, given that Clinton's implicature is clearly inferable, we can assume that to ignore it was an intentional discursive strategy. That is, by combating Clinton's utterance with "No, no," Trump displays negative epistemic stance towards the explicit content of her just prior claim, adding on an account of why her "plan" should not be considered as such by stating "you're telling the enemy everything you want to do." Therefore, although the content of Trump's turn in line 6 is a reiteration of his previous assertion in line 1, by responding directly to Clinton's just previous turn, it not only communicates negative evaluative stance towards Clinton's ISIS strategy, but also makes salient a direct juxtaposition of epistemic stance, with Trump displaying negative epistemic stance towards the view that Clinton's strategy can be considered a "plan." It is only in line 7 that Clinton refutes Trump's statement, thereby communicating negative epistemic stance towards the claim that she's "telling the enemy everything [she wants] to do"; however, this stance contradicts her previous positive epistemic stance towards Trump's statement that her plan is on her website that she had implicitly aligned herself with in line 4.

In this extract, we see both Clinton and Trump performing analogous discursive strategies, namely (a) communicating strong implicatures to discredit the other's political strategies, and (b) ignoring interpretations of the other's utterance that are unfavorable to them. However, the difference between the two political actors lies in the way they responded to the strong implicatures of the other. Clinton's negative evaluative stance towards Trump's lack of plan is only communicated implicitly in line 4, thus leaving open the explicit content of her utterance as a target for Trump's next utterance; this he capitalizes on in line 6, both diverting attention from her implicit criticism while at the same time calling into question the legitimacy of her just prior utterance. Trump, on the other hand, when faced with an analogous strategy from Clinton in line 4, ignores her strong implicature that he doesn't have a plan. Instead, he responds to the explicit content of her utterance directly in line 6, which itself communicates no salient alternative interpretation. Clinton's next move is thus to respond to the only available interpretation left open, namely the criticism of her ISIS plan.

4.3. Disaffiliation of stance by exploiting strong implicatures

In this final extract, we see a slightly different strategy employed by Clinton, namely of orienting to a strongly inferable implicature of the other candidate for her own purposes. The topic leading up to extract (3) is whether the candidates believe the police to be implicitly biased based on race, which leads Trump to open a discussion of how the African-American community has been "let down by our politicians."

(3)

1 TRUMP	And I will tell you, you look at the inner cities–and I just left Detroit, and I just left Philadelphia, and I just–you know, you've seen me, I've been all over the place
2	You decided to stay home, and that's OK
3	But I will tell you, I've been all over
4	and I've met some of the greatest people I'll ever meet within these communities
5	and they are very, very, upset with what their politicians have told them and what their politicians have done
6 HOLT	Mr Trump, I –
7 CLINTON	I think–I think –
8	I think Donald just criticized me for preparing for this debate
9	And yes I did

10	And you know what else I prepared for? I prepared to be president. And I think that's a good thing
11	[AUDIENCE APPLAUSE]

Having made reference to his recent travels in line 1, in line 2, Trump draws a comparison with Clinton's lack of travels, charging her with her decision "to stay home," both highlighting her agency in her lack of action, while also making an explicit value judgment on that decision by stating "and that's OK." However, by juxtaposing his own travels with Clinton's absence, his remark carries an ironic, facetious tone. As such, he strongly implicates his negative evaluative stance that staying home was not "OK," in turn implicating that Clinton does not have the firsthand experience of discussing relevant issues with the electorate as he does.

Trump continues describing his interactions with the people he has met in lines 3 to 6, at which point Clinton interrupts the moderator to make her own comment from line 7. Specifically, in line 8, Clinton orients to Trump's strong implicature made in line 2, acknowledging that his earlier turn was a criticism of her (lack of) action. In this way, she operationalizes Trump's implicit meaning, confirming a shared understanding of his utterance. However, rather than admit Trump's negative assessment based on the alleged misguided lack of action, she instead implicitly criticizes Trump for accusing her of taking the (presumably desirable) action of "preparing for this debate." In turn, she communicates her own implicature that–since Trump did not stay home as she did–he did not prepare for the debate, thus also implicitly communicating negative evaluative stance towards his actions of having "been all over the place." In this way, her utterance in line 8 plays a dual role of (a) reframing the content of Trump's implicit criticism against Clinton in a positive light, thereby calling into question the appropriateness of his making the criticism in the first place, and (b) implicitly communicating her own negative evaluative stance towards Trump's lack of preparations.

Clinton goes a step further. She confirms the content of the alleged "criticism" in line 9 ("and yes I did") thus asserting her positive epistemic stance towards her own actions of preparing for the debate, before posing a rhetorical question, "and you know what else I prepared for?," which she immediately answers with "I prepared to be president." Again, this comment strongly communicates both explicit and implicit content, on the one hand emphasizing her own desirable actions of preparing for the presidency (which is confirmed by her follow up, "and I think that's a good thing"), while at the same time implicitly, but no less strongly, casting aspersions on Trump's fitness for office by strongly implicating that he has not prepared to be president as she has.

Unlike in the previous extract where we saw both Trump and Clinton ignoring negatively framed implicatures of the other, in this extract, we see Clinton exploiting Trump's negatively framed implicature by both acknowledging it but at the same time disaligning herself from its negative evaluative stance by revising the content of the alleged criticism to show herself in a positive light. Moreover, by revising the evaluative stance from negative to positive, she also implicitly communicates her own strongly recoverable implicature juxtaposing her own positive action against Trump's, thereby communicating negative evaluative stance towards his presidential preparations.

5. Concluding remarks

This chapter has contributed to the study of stance in political discourse by demonstrating how implicatures–as implicit aspects of meaning inferable from a given utterance–can be targeted as the object of a stance act to promote one's own political stance. Focusing on the institutional context of political debate, it has examined the use of implicatures in interactional data obtained from the 2016 US presidential debates, in which two US politicians from two different parties, Donald Trump and Hillary Clinton, interacted with each other and their audiences.

While stance is typically thought of in terms of displaying an attitude or positioning oneself towards propositional content, this chapter has demonstrated that the expression of propositional content can itself be a way of (a) communicating stance, (b) negotiating stance as co-constructed among interlocutors, and, crucially, (c) manipulating the expression of stance of other interlocutors. But moreover, it has shown how stance as a public act can be expressed via indirect means, exposing how implicatures–while typically thought of in terms of propositional content–play the role of expressing attitudes towards another's content. That is, this chapter has shown how adding implicatures to our arsenal of explanatory tools offers a new way of understanding the complexity of the public act of stancetaking, providing a novel insight into the interactional function of implicatures and how they can be manipulated for the purpose of drawing attention to and supporting one's own personal and political motives.

Through the analysis of Trump and Clinton's interactions, I have identified three ways in which an interlocutor can draw on the inferable meanings of the other to promote their own stance. First, I showed how explicit meanings with negative consequences for one party can be reframed as negative charges against the other, thereby pitting one another's stance against each other. However, without explicitly denying the charges, this strategy comes with the possibly unfortunate consequence of implicitly aligning oneself with the content posed by the other. Next, I demonstrated how a similar strategy can be adopted by ignoring unwanted implicatures of the other, even when these implicatures are clearly intended and strongly inferable, instead acknowledging and/or responding to explicit content. The benefit of this discursive move is that it orients the interaction away from unfavorable comments directed at oneself, while at the same time allowing one to discredit the stance of the other found in the explicit content of a previous utterance. Nevertheless, this strategy also comes with a warning: by communicating a jibe in the implicit content of an utterance, it leaves open the explicit content as the target for future communicative attack. The final extract showed a slightly different way of dealing with negatively framed implicatures of the other, namely of acknowledging the implicature and hence operationalizing that meaning, but also of reframing its content in order to show oneself in a positive light. All in all, this brief survey of discursive strategies has demonstrated how the object of stance can be found in the implicit content of a previous turn, while at the same time it has shown how stance itself can be communicated implicitly, but no less publicly.

While this chapter has contributed to the study of stance by introducing implicature as an explanatory tool, from the other side of the coin, namely from the perspective of philosophical pragmatics, this chapter has also provided a more nuanced account of how the multiplicity of meanings that are inferable from a single utterance can be targeted in future turns, whether they are explicit meanings pertaining to uttered sentence forms, or salient meanings that are (sometimes implicitly) communicated by interlocutors. This focus on the interactional relationship between sequential utterances has ramifications for understanding how propositional meanings are negotiated and co-constructed between communicative participants in observably patternable ways. While Elder and Haugh's (2018) account highlights that strongly inferable, intended meanings of a speaker may not be the ones that are picked up on by other interlocutors, the context of political debate has allowed us to take this idea further, as it has served to demonstrate how inferable meanings of another interlocutor can be used in communicatively deviant ways to support one's own preferred narrative or to discredit the views of another. So, by posing the manipulation of implicatures in terms of stance, we now have a more fine-grained understanding of the motivations for adopting different ways of manipulating implicatures as discursive strategies.

References

Arundale, R. B. (2013). Conceptualizing "interaction" in interpersonal pragmatics: Implications for understanding and research. *Journal of Pragmatics, 58*, 12-26.

Ausderan, J. (2020). Oh, that's just crazy talk: How leaders use language to create perceptions of irrationality. In L. N. Berlin (Ed.), *Positioning and stance in political discourse: The individual, the party, and the party line,* (pp. 55-69). Wilmington, DE: Vernon Press.

Berlin, L. N. (2012). The making of a new American revolution or a wolf in sheep's clothing: "It's time to reload." In L. N. Berlin & A. Fetzer (Eds.), *Dialogue in politics* (pp. 167-192). Amsterdam/Philadelphia: John Benjamins.

Berlin, L. N. (2020). The positioning of post-truth politics: Claims and evidence in the 2016 US Presidential Campaigns. In L. N. Berlin (Ed.), *Positioning and stance in political discourse: The individual, the party, and the party line,* (pp. 1-30). Wilmington, DE: Vernon Press.

Biber, D., & Finegan, E. (1988). Adverbial stance types in English. *Discourse Processes, 11* (1), 1-34.

Bond, G. D., Homan, R. D., Eggert, J-A. L., Speller, L. F., Garcia, O. N., Majia, S. C., McInnes, K. W., Ceniceros, E. C., & Rustige, R. (2017). "Lyin' Ted," "Crooked Hillary," and "Deceptive Donald": Language of lies in the 2016 US presidential debates. *Applied Cognitive Psychology, 31*, 668-677.

Chilton, P. (2004). *Analysing political discourse: Theory and practice.* London: Routledge.

Clift, R. (2006). Indexing stance: Reported speech as an interactional evidential. *Journal of Sociolinguistics, 10*, 569-595.

Drew, P. (1987). Po-faced receipts of teases. *Linguistics, 25* (1), 219-253.

DuBois, J. W. (2007). The stance triangle. In R. Englebretson (Ed.), *Stancetaking in discourse: Subjectivity, evaluation, interaction* (pp. 139-192). Amsterdam/Philadelphia: John Benjamins.

Elder, C. (2019). Negotiating what is said in the face of miscommunication. In P. Stalmaszczyk (Ed.), *Philosophical insights into pragmatics* (pp. 107-126). Berlin/Boston: De Gruyter.

Elder, C., & Haugh, M. (2018). The interactional achievement of speaker meaning: Toward a formal account of conversational inference. *Intercultural Pragmatics, 15*, 593-625.

Field, M. (1997). The role of factive predicates in the indexicalization of stance: A discourse perspective. *Journal of Pragmatics, 27* (6), 799-814.

Grice, P. (1975/1989). Logic and conversation. In P. Grice, *Studies in the way of words* (pp. 22-40). Cambridge, MA: Harvard University Press.

Grice, P. (1989). *Studies in the way of words.* Cambridge MA: Harvard University Press.

Hall, E. T. (1976). *Beyond culture.* New York: Anchor Books.

Haviland, J. B. (1991). "Sure, sure": Evidence and affect. *Text, 9*, 27-68.

Heritage, J., & Raymond, G. (2005). The terms of agreement: Indexing epistemic authority and subordination in talk-in-interaction. *Social Psychology Quarterly, 68*, 15-38.

Heylighen, F., & Dewaele, J.-M. (2002). Variation in the contextuality of language: An empirical measure. *Foundations of Science, 7*, 293-340.

Ibaños, A. M. T., Behle, N., & Penz, Y. (2020). Discarding proper names as referring expression tweets in the Trump vs. Hillary debate. In L. N. Berlin (Ed.), *Positioning and stance in political discourse: The individual, the party, and the party line*, (pp. 93-107). Wilmington, DE: Vernon Press.

Internet Archive. (2016). Political TV Ad Archive: Debate Project. Retrieved March 25, 2019, from http://politicaladarchive.org/debate-project/.

Jaffe, A. (2009). The sociolinguistics of stance. In A. Jaffe (Ed.), *Stance: Sociolinguistic perspectives* (pp. 3-28). Oxford: Oxford University Press.

Kampf, Z. (2016). All the best! Performing solidarity in political discourse. *Journal of Pragmatics, 93*, 47-60.

Kärkkäinen, E. (2003). *Epistemic stance in English conversation: A description of its interactional functions, with a focus on I think.* Amsterdam/Philadelphia: John Benjamins.

Katz, A. J. (2016, October 24). The Presidential Debates Set Ratings Records in 2016. Retrieved Retrieved January 31, 2020, from https://www.adweek.com/tv-video/presidential-debates-set-ratings-records-2016-does-format-need-change-174205/.

Keisanen, T. (2007). Stancetaking as an interactional activity: Challenging the prior speaker. In R. Englebretson (Ed.), *Stancetaking in discourse: Subjectivity, evaluation, interaction*, (pp. 253-281). Amsterdam/Philadelphia: John Benjamins.

Kiesling, S. F. (2009). Style as stance. In A. Jaffe (Ed.), *Stance: Sociolinguistic perspectives* (pp. 171-194). Oxford: Oxford University Press.

Koshik, I. (2003). Wh-questions used as challenges. *Discourse Studies, 5*, 51-77.

Luscombe, R. (2016, October 1). Hillary Clinton calls Trump "temperamentally unfit" to lead after Machado spat. Retrieved January 31, 2020, from https://www.theguardian.com/us-news/2016/sep/30/clinton-trump-temperamentally-unfit-lead-alicia-machado.

Martín de la Rosa, V., Domínguez Romero, E., Pérez Blanco, M., & Marín-Arrese, J. I. (2020). Epistemic and effective stance in political discourse: The European refugee crisis. In L. N. Berlin (Ed.), *Positioning and stance in political discourse: The individual, the party, and the party line*, (pp. 141-156). Wilmington, DE: Vernon Press.

Nuolijärvi, P., & Tiittula, L. (2011). Irony in political television debates. *Journal of Pragmatics, 43* (2), 572-587.

Ochs, E. (1996). Linguistic resources for socializing humanity. In J. J. Gumperz & S. C. Levinson (Eds.), *Rethinking linguistic relativity* (pp. 407-437). Cambridge: Cambridge University Press.

Ochs, E., & Schieffelin, B. (1989). Language has a heart. *Text, 9* (1), 7-25.

Prieto-Mendoza, M. A. (2020). Positioning in the peace process: Stance during the Colombian Peace Dialogues. In L. N. Berlin (Ed.), *Positioning and stance in political discourse: The individual, the party, and the party line*, (pp. 31-53). Wilmington, DE: Vernon Press.

Reyes, A. (2015). Building intimacy through linguistic choices, text structure and voices in political discourse. *Journal of Pragmatics, 43*, 58-71.

Sacks, H., Schegloff, E. A., & Jefferson, G. (1974). A simplest systematics for the organization of turn-taking for conversation. *Language, 50* (4), 696-735.

Schallhorn, K. (2018, August 13). Trump's nicknames for rivals, from "Rocket Man" to "Pocahontas." Retrieved January 31, 2020, from https://www.foxnews.com/politics/trumps-nicknames-for-rivals-from-rocket-man-to-pocahontas.

Schegloff, E. A. (1981). Discourse as an interactional achievement: Some uses of uh huh and other things that come between sentences. In D. Tannen (Ed.), *Analyzing discourse: Text and talk* (pp. 71-93). Washington: Georgetown University Press.

Walker, M. A. (1996). Inferring acceptance and rejection in dialog by default rules of inference. *Language and Speech, 39* (2-3), 265-304.

Chapter 5

Discarding Proper Names as Referring Expression Tweets in the Trump vs. Hillary Debate

Ana Maria Tramunt Ibaños, Nanashara Behle, & Yuri Penz
Pontifícia Universidade Católica do Rio Grande do Sul, Porto Alegre, Brasil

Abstract

Our chapter deals with the use of definite expressions, adjective, or adjective-like markers to refer to people on Twitter as a way of taking a stance in favor of or against somebody. We exemplify our research with tweets about the first debate of the two US presidential candidates. Our first findings have shown that some descriptions, such as "thin-skinned bully," "mediocre male," "Mrs. Bill Clinton," "the woman that was cheated on," tend to be repeated by followers in a way of undermining the arguments for or against the candidates. This type of stance is grammatically embedded either as an argument or a predicative in a 140-character message. Our hypothesis is that these definite descriptions are what matters in this type of argument, guided by the evaluative attitude displayed by actors.

1. Introduction

As it is well known, Twitter provides an easy form of communication that enables users to broadcast and share information about their activities, opinions, and status (Java, Song, Finin, & Tseng, 2007). According to Cha, Haddadi, Benevenuto, and Gummadi (2010), there are three "interpersonal" activities on Twitter: (a) users interact by following updates of people who post interesting tweets; (b) users can pass along interesting pieces of information to their followers, and (c) users can respond to (or comment on) other people's tweets. And it is possible to evaluate a Twitter account by its indegree influence (Riquelme & González-Cantergiani, 2016); that is, the number of followers of a user directly indicating the size of the audience; its retweet influence, which is measured by the number of retweets containing one's name, indicating the ability of that user to generate content with some kind of value, and its mention influence, which is measured by the number of mentions containing one's name, indicating the ability of that user to engage others in a conversation.

In our work, we follow Tumasjan, Sprenger, Sandner, and Welpe (2010) in the sense of considering Twitter as a platform for political deliberation, or at least a platform for spreading or discussing political ideas or preferences.

Let us assume that an individual's act potentially leads others to engage in a certain act. With this in mind, our purpose is to analyze Twitter interactions related to the first presidential debate between Donald Trump and Hillary Clinton, to examine the way people on Twitter take a stance in favor of or against one or both presidential candidates. More specifically, we aim to study the use of referring expressions in tweets and pragmatically analyze the weight the choice of determined referring expressions have on the content of a tweet. In other words, the focus is on the choice actors make in terms of using definite expressions, adjective, or adjective-like markers instead of proper names, to refer both candidates. To do so, we make use of a threefold interface: cyberpragmatics, politeness (Yus, 2001; 2008; 2011) and referring expressions (Costa, 2004).

In his works on cyberpragmatics, Yus (2011) points out that rules for *netiquette* (e.g., respect different opinions, avoid formal language, read the rules of the social network, sign messages, and avoid offensive messages) is forgotten and Internet-mediated communication (IMC) becomes a realm where politeness or lack thereof marks the relevance (Sperber & Wilson, 1986/1995) of the communication. These ideas of Relevance Theory are based on the work of Grice (1989), which show that expectations are automatically created by utterances, making it possible for the receptor to understand the speaker's meaning. Yus (2001; 2011) uses the principles of Relevance Theory in his studies: the Cognitive Principle of Relevance that explains that human cognition tends toward the maximization of relevance, and the Communicative Principle of Relevance which is about the expectations of an optimal relevance of an ostensive stimulus (Sperber & Wilson, 1986/1995). An individual joins a group according to their choices, knowing that these groups are, most of the time, pseudo communities. And although we can only create hypotheses about whom we are talking to, conversational strategies on Twitter are not so different from face to face conversational strategies. Besides, Twitter gives us the possibility of remaining in a group or not (Rheingold, 1993).

The study of proper name, definite description, and attributive or referential interpretations has been the object of semantic and philosophical contentiousness since the Frege vs. Russell debate (Russell, 1971), and has permeated a great number of theories that deal with reference (Donellan, 1966/1972; Kripke, 1980; Salmon, 1981; Soames, 1986). Although our work deals with the use of proper names or substitutes for them in tweets, we based our analysis on a pragmatic approach presented by Campos (1992) and Costa (2004) in which he discusses the implicatures and inferences triggered by the choice of words used to refer to someone. Ibaños and Behle (in press) also make use of this theoretical apparatus to discuss references in tweets.

Summing up, referring is a part of communicating, and communication is essentially a transmission of knowledge (Evans, 1982). One chooses to enable one's audience to think of or focus on the intended object (Bach, 2004; cf. Berlin, this volume; Martín de la Rosa, Domínguez Romero, Pérez Blanco, & Marín-Arrese, this volume; Prieto-Mendoza, this volume), no matter the opinion they are going to support.

2. Referring Expressions

Referring expressions constitute some of the most ordinary phenomena in the everyday usage of natural language. This specific phenomenon establishes the very core of the semantic/pragmatic process of referring, conveyed between some linguistic entity (i.e., any entry one may consider as a simple or complex constituent) and its corresponding reference in the world. Concerning syntax, coreference plays a major role in anaphors, with no regard to reference as it is to be understood in the field of semantics:

(1) John$_i$ says he$_i$ is far too impatient for this year to be over.
(2) John$_i$ says he$_j$ wants to spend the whole holiday traveling abroad.
(3) #He$_i$ says John$_i$ is loving the new city!

Examples (1) and (2) display different entities for coreference, according to the index following the proper name and the pronoun, although (3) is considered ungrammatical, for there is no language in the world in which the pronoun may be co-referred by the proper name, postponed in a way that they both indicate the same entity in the world.

Many years before the Chomskyan turn would become a genuine Copernican revolution within the study and the theories of language, Frege (1892/1980; 1884/1953) was already concerned with the relationship between a proper name, *Plato*, for example, and a certain definite description, *the professor of Aristotle*, for instance. We can saturate such a proposition by composing it as (4) below in order to predicate over the argument:

(4) Plato was the professor of Aristotle.

However, even though one is allowed to affirm correctly that such a proposition is true, one is also authorized to question in which circumstances the definite description, also assumed here as a referring expression, could replace a proper name. Certainly, although Plato could have been widely referred to as the professor of Aristotle, he has not been so for his entire life, precisely because during Plato's childhood he was not even a professor, yet he was still Plato.

Deeply concerned with the syntax of argument/predicate composition, Frege had to assume any kind of expression in the position of an unsaturated argument was a proper name, like (5), independently of (6):

(5) The professor of Aristotle was Greek.
(6) Plato was Greek.

Anything one can refer to in the world can be used as a proper name then, overpopulating the so-called realm of proper names.

Some years after, Russell (1919; 1971) did the very opposite, emptying out the realm of proper names by assuming the only logically genuine proper names are the pronouns "this" or "that," relegating ordinary proper names people usually deal with to some sort of "dummy" proper names. "John" and "Mary," for instance, play a role within natural language, behaving as if they were real proper names by means of the *acquaintance* notion, only because of the properties of acknowledgment and familiarity that speakers establish between ordinary proper names and entities in the world, lacking a particular meaning. What does "Donald Trump" mean, for instance? Certainly not "the President of United States" in logical terms, even though this definite description fits the reference for Trump nowadays.

Criticizing the entire enterprise of descriptivism represented by the large work of Frege and Russell, Kripke (1980) refreshes the discussion concerning proper names versus definite descriptions as referring expressions by means of introducing his Causal Theory of Reference, sustained by a modal logic institution of his own.

Kripke (1980) identifies proper names as rigid designators; that is, proper names are a very unique way to identify certain individuals in any possible world in which we may refer to them. Hillary Clinton, for instance, could have had many different lives other than being presidential candidate for the United States. She could have been a physics professor or a car saleswoman, a Spanish politician, or anything else. All of these possible predicative states of affairs could assign what properties Hillary Clinton would possess in each of these worlds. There is no such world, however, in which Hillary Clinton is not Hillary Clinton, mainly because the proper name rigidly designates the individual in any possible world.

The causal chain established between proper names and definite descriptions within Kripke's framework (1980) specifies that there is a sort of connection between the initial "baptism" through which a rigid designator refers to an individual in any possible world and all the uses, mentions, and references to that name in this same world. Besides, the most prominent definite descriptions may be assigned to a certain name which conveys a rigid designator for it in any world in such a way that we may be able to identify some individuals due to their historical recognition in the actual world, such as "the first Queen of England" or "the Father of Jesus." However, it is *Mary* and *Joseph* that rigidly designate the individuals in any world we may talk about, even in some counterfactual worlds in which they had nothing to do with the monarchy or Christianity and so on.

Campos (1992) and Costa (2004) offer insights for the study of the philosophy of language and the philosophy of linguistics, mainly in terms of proper names as complex entities of meaning and reference in natural language. The author develops a proposal for the study of proper names and referring expressions in which there are two ways of analyzing them: (a) from a logico-semantic point of view and (b) from a communicative-pragmatic point of view.

Campos (1992) and Costa (2004) propose an adaptation of Kripke's insight concerning the very phenomenon of reference within such a framework contending that semantic reference corresponds to a relation between referring expressions and referents the same way as pragmatic reference deals with reference and speaker's reference. In this chapter, we attempt to conjoin semantic and pragmatic phenomena of reference, interacting between the domains of referent, referring expressions, and speaker's reference.

3. Politeness and cyberpragmatics

Social networks have been increasingly used by people to express their opinions not only to friends, but also to the whole chosen community on these platforms. Apparently, the participants of a communication process follow the same kind of rules in real and in virtual life. However, they are protected by the distance and anonymity the Internet setting provides, thus contributing to breaking rules of politeness (Brown & Levinson, 1987) freely, known as netiquette when applied to virtual social networks.

In addition to the maintenance of good communicational coexistence, it is also important to think about how the understanding between interlocutors occurs. When a statement is posted on the Internet, it can be received by countless numbers of people who do not always possess the common references expected by the author for the desired interpretation of the text.

Unlike face to face communication, Internet communication does not convey facial expressions, tone of voice, etc., all of which are key to a more accurate understanding of someone's expressed ideas.[1] This type of communication can, then, be impaired, lacking resources that could either help understanding inferences conveyed by the author of the tweet or mislead the outcome of a conversation. As already pointed out elsewhere, we follow notions of cyberpragmatics and Internet-mediated communication (Yus, 2001; 2011), which we will briefly discuss in this section, along with politeness. Both ideas, politeness and cyberpragmatics, are based on inferential pragmatic theories. The first uses Grice's Theory of Implicatures and the second, Relevance Theory as proposed by Sperber and Wilson (1986/1995; Wilson & Sperber, 2005), which in turn also relies on Gricean concepts.

Brown and Levinson (1987) state that politeness is compatible with the Cooperative Principle and the maintenance of conversational maxims, presented by Grice (1975). The idea is that the interlocutors must be engaged in the same principles in a communicative process to achieve a successful conversational result. Grice also points out that the Cooperative Principle engages four categories of conversational supermaxims (quantity, quality, manner, and relation) which will guarantee a successful communication. However, when at least one of the supermaxims is violated, an implicature must be generated through an inferential process so that the statement can be understood.

Brown and Levinson (1987) associate politeness with Grice's supermaxim of manner, identified simply as "be polite." But they also point out that all social interaction is potentially face-threatening; thus, adhering to the Cooperative Principle helps maintain harmony and understanding in an interaction. In the course of this process, the interlocutors try to preserve a good image of themselves and preserve the other's adherence to the Cooperative Principle. This public reputation that the participants try to maintain is what Brown and Levinson (1987) refer to as "face." It is established during interlocution and therefore can be preserved, improved, or lost.

The acts that Brown and Levinson (1987) believe may threaten the face of an interlocutor seem to be consistent in face-to-face communication and in virtual communication. The authors classify these acts; (a) threatening the speaker's positive face; and (b) threatening the speaker's negative face. Examples of face-threatening acts under (a) are criticisms, contradictions, disagreement, challenges, irreverence, and other kinds of conflicts. Face-threatening acts under (b) include orders and requests, suggestions and

---

[1] Thanks to Jacob Ausderan for this idea and many others.

advice, reminders, warnings, promises, and praise. Threats in category (a) occur during an apology, admission of praise, emotional disorder, and similar acts. And threats to the speaker's negative face (b) occur through acts of thanks, admission of thanks or apologies, etc. We can see that all these notions of threats to the face of both the listener and the speaker (and we can consider other types of interlocutors, as in the case of social networks) corroborate Brown and Levinson's notion that all kinds of conversational acts have the potential to alter the image of the communicator or the receiver, or both. In addition, etiquette and politeness rules, which do not rely solely on linguistic attributes, are necessary to reduce "noise" and misunderstanding. In the case of Internet-based communication, the choice of words, expressions, and emoticons may be perceived as threatening to some, but may be seen as creating solidarity among others. This is explored by Yus (2011), in terms of cyberpragmatics.

Cyberpragmatics is anchored in an inferential pragmatic perspective based on the Relevance Theory (Sperber & Wilson, 1986/1995; Wilson & Sperber, 2005). Yus (2001; 2008; 2011) suggests that the receiver analyzes the logical form of a statement and constructs the propositional form through inferential processes, while obtaining implicit or explicit information. The cyberpragmatics approach shows how information is used and interpreted in the specific context of the Internet, as well as analyzes how participants in the communication process use the contextual clues to fill in the gaps left between what is posted and what the user really wants to communicate.

For Yus (2001; 2011), the user of a virtual platform (a) chooses which social group they will join on the Internet, (b) selects between one group or another, and (c) establishes an intragroup identity. In virtual communities, there may be shared trivial and/or profound aspects concerning everyday life that may not be taken for granted or assumed as unnecessary *a priori*. We cannot conceive of virtual communities in the same way we perceive real communities because concepts of place, cognition, and social processes are not always shared; therefore, virtual environments are called "pseudo communities" (Yus, 2011). In these pseudo communities, users are expected to be involved in a virtual discussion, having access to a specific context. But, as the author points out, in the case of mediated communication on the Internet, we need to evaluate how the quality of the information and the positioning of the virtual interlocutors will have an impact on the balance of cognitive effects in order to reach optimal relevance.

Yus (2008) also argues that web-based conversational strategies do not differ from face-to-face conversation, in that network interlocutors also hypothesize the existence and scope of the mutually-manifest cognitive environment as an essential element for the interaction. In this way, the principles of relevance are used to explain the functioning of the communicative process in the approach of cyberpragmatics. In Relevance Theory (Sperber & Wilson, 1986/1995; Wilson & Sperber, 2005), the two guiding principles are the cognitive principle of relevance and the communicative principle of relevance. The first states that the human mind seeks to maximize relevance in communication, and the second indicates that an ostensive stimulus communicates the intention of optimal relevance.

Summarizing, Internet-mediated communication in context is the main notion of cyberpragmatics (Yus, 2001; 2011) and its connection to relevance is made in Yus (2011). According to the study, speakers display communicative intentions as they expect their utterances to be relevant, demonstrating a degree of intentionality towards the audience, enabling a well-interpreted communication by means of a cost/benefit measure. The Internet users use inference strategies to interpret messages, and it is not different from face-to-face communication. The author relates this to the cognitive principle of relevance which points out the speakers' mind seeks the maximization for relevance. The users believe their receptors have access to the same contextual information that will allow the expected interpretation of the utterance. Each Internet platform influences the quality of user access to contextual information and therefore the cognitive effects and mental efforts are different for each of these tools.

Thus, the conditions of relevance on the Web postulated by Yus (2001; 2011) are that the information generated is relevant to an individual whenever the social benefit obtained for their social network is high. In addition, the information generated is socially relevant to an individual whenever the effort required to produce and transmit it does not invalidate the satisfaction that the user obtained by presenting such information in their social networks. A cost and benefit balance between cognitive effect and mental efforts is required to obtain optimal communication.

As for the microblogging tool, Twitter, the platform from which we collected our corpus of data, Yus (2001; 2011) makes some relevant considerations, pointing out that the use of this type of tool responds to the human need to connect with other users and know what they are doing. However, microblogging is unique because it only allows short messages,[2] which allows for greater speed in the updates and interactions between users. Within a pragmatic perspective, Yus (2011) states that the goal of cyberpragmatics–evaluating the quality of interactions–is pertinent in a platform such as Twitter since the basic premise of this media tool is to answer the question

---

[2] At the time of the presidential debate between Clinton and Trump, only 140 characters were possible per tweet whereas 280 characters are possible currently.

"What are you doing?" At first, the answers seem to offer irrelevant statements, but the study points out that there are probably other ways to reward the efforts made by the Twitter interlocutors. One of the reasons might be a "caring environment" that the number of messages and intimacy provides to the users, since the users will make inferences that the communicators intend to share their activities. In addition, the study suggest that the generalities of information supposedly serve to establish a mutual cognitive environment among users.

4. Methodology

The corpus of our analysis is composed of tweets published during the First Presidential Debate (2016). As it was considered the most-tweeted debate ever (there were 17.1 million interactions on Twitter about the event, according to Nielsen's Social Content Ratings), we collected 4 tweets and their response tweets from different actors from each side of the political spectrum to evaluate the choices they made in terms of deleting the candidates' names and substituting them for definite expressions, adjective or adjective-like markers. As an empirical study, the number of tweets is not especially relevant because tweets represent the collective ideas of groups, not necessarily individuals. These tweets were deemed important because they received a great number of responses, either supporting or challenging their ideas. The analysis, then, focused on referring expressions and adjectives in the extended exchanges.

5. Analyses

As mentioned previously, we examined the substitution of proper names for definite descriptions in evaluative expressions used in tweets in such a way that the audience understands who is being referred to by the utterance. Our aim was to evaluate the optimal relevance (Sperber & Wilson, 1986/1995) through the lens of cyberpragmatics (Yus, 2001; 2008; 2011).

The discarding of proper names on the microblogging server may occur to fulfill the need to follow the established rules of etiquette on the Internet, or to fulfill the principle raised by Yus of causing some specific effect that would allow the realization of pragmatic inferences of the implicature type (Elder, this volume; Grice, 1975). Some etiquette rules on the Internet are related to the conversational maxims as proffered by Grice, including "Do not make your contribution to the conversation more informative than necessary" and "be brief." Being brief is a requirement on Twitter due to the limitation of characters per message (140 characters). If we consider the people involved in this kind of process (the tweeters), they are at least minimally engaged in the

Cooperative Principle; that is, the meaning that they intend to convey must occur within the pre-established limit.

Discarding proper names to preserve the character limit may be a deciding factor; however, in substituting referring expressions, the expression itself is sometimes even longer than the original name. In this case, it may be an intentional violation of a conversational maxim, as well as the breaking of etiquette rules, in order to avoid offense and discord. In addition, the use of definite descriptions with referential use (in Donellan's sense), can be the trigger of optimal relevance; that is, "every act of ostensive communication communicates a presumption of its own optimal relevance" (Sperber & Wilson, 1986/1995, p.158).

As specified in the introduction of this chapter, our purpose is to evaluate some tweets produced during the first debate between Hillary Clinton and Donald Trump in the race for the President of the United States of America on September 27, 2017, with the intent of exemplifying theoretical questions. The analyzed tweets were (a) written in English, and (b) representative of the disagreements between the protagonists in relation to their preferences for one candidate or another. The context, therefore, is the dispute between the two eligible candidates at the time of the production of theses tweets. It is this context that makes it feasible to understand the intention of the interlocutors and the possible inferred implicatures triggered in the tweets. As Twitter is (or may be) a means of real-time communication, it is possible that the relevance of the messages will be lost if they are read long after the fact; the noise of time may cause the utterance to lose its meaning or even to be inferred in a different way.

The examples (1) through (9) are representative of tweets, retweets, and likes of a single group with a strong influence on the levels (a) indegree (audience insights); (b) retweet; and (c) mention. None of them refer to the candidates by their names, but substitute expressions, such as "The thin-skinned bully," "good for nothing FLOTUS," "salesman," and "Our MAGA," which end up becoming references for the candidates which are repeated over several exchanges between the tweeters. Although the expression "Oval," metonymy of "White House" and therefore the American Government, is also recurrent in these tweets, it is not our focus in this paper.

(1) The thin-skinned bully doesn't care about anyone but himself
(2) In the real world, she was presidential and he was hysterical
(3) Do you want an underprepared individual in the Oval?
(4) This nation needs a statesman not a salesman
(5) Orange-faced man throws 90 minute tantrum while getting challenged by a powerful, poised, presidential woman

(6) The mediocre male's days may be numbered

(7) It was like putting a potzer up against a Kasparov to play chess

(8) This good for nothing FLOTUS won't have a chance.

(9) Our MAGA is by far the best candidate.

We chose four of the above tweets produced during debate for a detailed analysis.

Figure 5.1. Tweet 1

In Figure 5.1, this first tweet contains the following information: (a) "she was presidential" and (b) "he was hysterical." While there is no referential definite descriptions, such as proposed by Donnellan (1972) and modified by Campos (1992) for references where there is only one person with a determined description, the adjectives "presidential" and "hysterical" attribute qualities to the subjects and, through the qualities given, the receptor infers the stance and intention, of the actor. This is easily perceived as the adjective "presidential" conveys a positive quality, whereas "hysterical" points to a negative one. What makes it possible to retrieve the referents of the respective feminine and masculine pronouns is their predicate relationship within the given context. Therefore, the adjective "presidential" corresponds to Hillary Clinton and "hysterical" to Donald Trump. The decidability power of the pronouns "he" or "she" is more context-dependent than proper names or definite descriptions.

Considering the rules of etiquette on the web, this tweet shows a politeness violation since the actor directly characterizes one of the candidates in a negative way. Similarly, the use of adjectives to disqualify one of the candidates violates politeness in the tweet in Figure 5.2.

Figure 5.2. Tweet 2

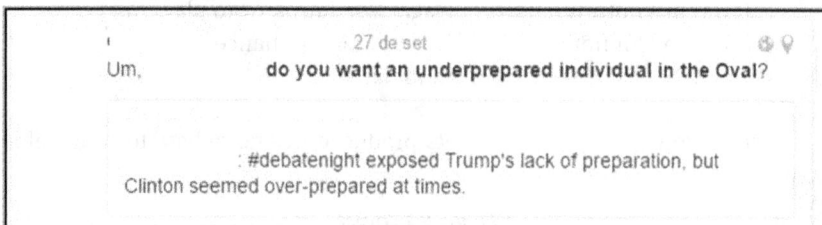

Um,   · 27 de set
                    do you want an underprepared individual in the Oval?

                    : #debatenight exposed Trump's lack of preparation, but
          Clinton seemed over-prepared at times.

In this second example, we have a tweet and a retweet (response). In the initial tweet, the tweeter produces a violation of manner by obscuring the referent in the expression "underprepared individual." We can only redeem her/his referent by going back to an earlier message where Trump is mentioned as the one who lacks preparation. In this way, apparently, the reference given by the author seems to have been understood.

In the second part–the response–characteristics that might otherwise appear be positive turn out to be negative. As such, a greater cognitive effort is required to reach the desired meaning of the author when s/he specifies "Trump's lack of preparation" and "Clinton seemed over-prepared." We would imagine that the lack of preparation of a candidate would generate an implicature like "The candidate is not suitable" and that the over-preparation would provide an implicature like "The candidate is suitable." However, the conjunction "but" shows the issuer's intention to make manifest the implicature "Neither candidate is suitable."

Figure 5.3. Tweet 3

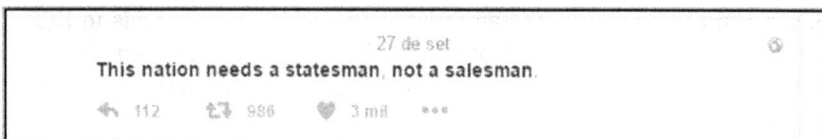

                              · 27 de set
          This nation needs a statesman, not a salesman.

      ↩ 112   ↻ 986   ♥ 3 mil   •••

In the third tweet presented in Figure 5.3, there is also the need for context to understand who the author means with the referring expressions. If we consider that the tweet has to do with the presidential debate, the gender of the noun might instantly elucidate whom the tweet is about. Furthermore, considering that Trump's work in the marketing world and media is widely known, the "salesman" reference also reveals the context and allows us to make implicatures for the understanding and rescue of the discarded proper name reference. From the tweet, we can retrieve the following: (a) the nation needs a statesman; (b) the nation does not need a salesman; (c) Trump is a salesman. Following syllogistic logic, such a retrieval authorizes the implicature "The nation does not need Trump" by characterizing the candidate as a salesman, a role which is not relevant for the needs of the nation.

Figure 5.4. Tweet 4

BREAKING: **Orange-faced man throws 90 minute tantrum while getting challenged** with facts **by a powerful, poised, presidential woman.** #debates

In the last example shown in Figure 5.4, the use of an expression that highlights physical attributes of one of the candidates, "Orange-faced," points to one of the most notorious and ridiculed features of Donald Trump's image on social networks. Once again, the context helps the readers to grasp the meaning of the expression and its referent, although his proper names haven't been mentioned. This appears to be the author's intention as s/he contrasts "Orange-faced man" with "powerful, poised, presidential woman."

The definite descriptions, as defined by the users in the examples above, exhibit a pragmatic reference which constitutes an identity throughout the tweets. Proper names lack sense (Kripke, 1980), but definite descriptions display certain properties implied by the authors of the communication (Campos, 1992). To call the presidential candidate "good for nothing FLOTUS" infers an axiological judgment over Hillary Clinton concerning her past as First Lady. Similarly, to refer to Donald Trump as a salesman relates to his identity as a real state entrepreneur, which has nothing to do with politicals.

6. Conclusion

The purpose of the study was to analyze tweets issued during the first presidential candidate debate between Hillary Clinton and Donald Trump in terms of a semantic-pragmatic approach mainly based on the study of proper names and referring expressions using pragmatic theory (Costa, 2004) and cyberpragmatics (Yus, 2001; 2011). Our findings have demonstrated that some descriptions, such as "thin-skinned bully"; "mediocre male"; "Mrs. Bill Clinton"; and "the woman that was cheated," tend to be repeated by followers in order to undermine the arguments for or against the candidates. This type of stance is grammatically embedded, either as an argument or a predicative, within the 140-character message. Guided by the evaluative attitude indicated within the tweets, our conclusion is that these referring expressions are what matters in advancing the stance of the authors.

References

Bach, K. (2004) Minding the Gap. In C. Bianchi (Ed.), *The semantics/pragmatics distinction* (pp. 27-43). Stanford: CSLI Publications.

Campos, J. (1992). Referência semântica–Referência pragmática: Sob Kripke. *Letras de Hoje, 27* (3), 11-24.

Cha, M., Haddadi, H., Benevenuto, F., & Gummadi, K. P. (2010). Measuring user influence in Twitter: The million-follower fallacy. In *Proceedings of the Fourth International AAAI Conference on Weblogs and Social Media* (pp. 10-17). Washington: George Washington University.

Costa, J. C. da (2004). *Os enigmas do nome: Na interface lógica/semântica/pragmática.* Porto Alegre: EdiPUCRS.

Donnellan, K. S. (1972). Proper names and identifying descriptions. In D. Davidson & G. Harman (Eds.), *Semantics of natural language* (pp. 356-378). Dordrecht, Holland: D. Reidel.

Elder, C. (2020). Trump vs. Clinton: Implicatures as public stance acts. In L. N. Berlin (Ed.), *Positioning and stance in political discourse: The individual, the party, and the party line,* (pp. 71-91). Wilmington, DE: Vernon Press."

Evans, G. (1982). *The varieties of reference* (J. McDowell, Ed.). Oxford: Clarendon Press.

Frege, G. (1892/1980). On sense and reference. In P. Geach and M. Black (Eds. & M. Black, Trans.), *Translations from the philosophical writings of Gottlob Frege* (3rd ed.) (pp. 56-78). Oxford: Blackwell.

Frege, G. (1884/1953). *Foundations of arithmetic* (J. L. Austin, Trans.). Oxford: Blackwell.

Grice, H. P. (1975). Logic and conversation. In P. Cole & J. L. Morgan (Eds.), *Speech acts: Syntax and semantics, Vol. 3* (pp. 41-58). New York: Academic.

Ibaños, A. M. T., & Behle, N. F. (in press). Nome próprio x descrição definida: Um estudo sobre etiqueta e relevância na Internet. Manuscript submitted for publication.

Java, A., Song, X., Finin, T., & Tseng B. (2007). Why we twitter: Understanding microblogging usage and communities. In 9th WebKDD and 1st SNA-KDD 2007 Workshop on Web mining and Social Network Analysis (pp. 56–65). https://doi.org/10.1145/1348549.1348556.

Kripke, S. (1980). *Naming and necessity.* Oxford: Basil Blackwell.

Riquelme, F., & González-Cantergiani, P. (2016). Measuring user influence in Twitter: A survey. *Information Processing & Management, 52* (5), 949-975.

Russell, B. (1919). *Introduction to mathematical philosophy.* London, UK: George Allen and Unwin.

Russell, B. (1971). On denoting. In R. C. Marsh (Ed.), *Bertrand Russell: Logic and knowledge: Essays 1901-1950* (pp. 39-56). New York: G. P. Putnam's Sons.

Salmon, N. U. (1981). *Reference and essence.* Princeton, NJ: Princeton University Press.

Soames, S. (1986). Incomplete definite descriptions. *Notre Dame Journal of Formal Logic, 27* (3), 349-375.

Sperber, D., & Wilson, D. (1986/1995). *Relevance: Communication and cognition.* Oxford: Blackwell.

Tumasjan, A., Sprenger, T. O., Sandner, P. G., & Welpe, I. M. (2010). Predicting elections with Twitter: What 140 characters reveal about political sentiment. In *Proceedings of the Fourth International AAAI Conference on Weblogs and Social Media* (pp. 178-185). Washington: George Washington University.

Wilson, D., & Sperber, D. (2005). Reply to Rajagopalan. *Intercultural Pragmatics, 2* (1), 99-103.

Yus, F. (2001). *Ciberpragmática: El uso del lenguaje en Internet.* Barcelona: Ariel.

Yus, F. (2008). Alterations of relevance in cyber-media. *Universitas Psychologica, 7* (3), 623-632.

Yus, F. (2011). *Cyberpragmatics: Internet-mediated communication in context.* Amsterdam/Philadelphia: John Benjamins.

Chapter 6

Stance in Casting the Identity of a New Political Leader: Interviews with the President of Argentina

Alejandro Parini* and Luisa Granato**
*University of Belgrano, Buenos Aires, Argentina
**Universidad Nacional de La Plata, Argentina

Abstract

This chapter looks at the construction of political identity through the adoption of different stances in the context of a series of political interviews with the former President of Argentina, Mauricio Macri, when he was first elected. The aim is to analyze the linguistic and discourse resources used by the President in the stancetaking process and with a view to evoking and constructing the identity of a new political leader. We argue that this construction of identity is framed within a contrastive rhetorical structure that is repeatedly employed by the President in his answers to the questions posed by the interviewers on different political shows aired on Argentinian television.

1. Introduction

In the political arena, citizens increasingly want to see that politicians are held accountable for their actions, and politicians themselves are increasingly under pressure from society to project nice and decent personae through appeals to approachability, informality, and emotionality (Lakoff, 2005). This is done mostly in different kinds of media settings, which offer the opportunity to address both mediated and/or unmediated audiences.

One such setting is the political interview. Political interviews, as instances of institutional public discourses aimed "to preserve a democratic political culture" (Andone, 2013, p. 103), constitute a mediated fertile arena in which politicians convey their political opinions regarding societal issues and thus present themselves as committed to their different endeavors as public servants. In this context, the identity of the interviewee as a political figure is manifested through his discursive performance aimed at both the interviewers and a mediated audience. Thus, identity can be conceived as being socially constructed in interaction (Benwell & Stoke, 2007; de Fina, Schiffrin, & Bamberg, 2006).

Against this background and taking as a departure point DuBois' (2007) conceptualization of stance as encompassing the acts of evaluation, positioning, and alignment, in this work we examine how the president of Argentina, Mauricio Macri, adopts and negotiates stance in a series of televised interviews that provide a context for the construction of his identity as a new political leader.

We argue that in the President's responses to the interviewers' questions, identity work is done chiefly by means of the rhetorical strategy of contrasting his government policies with those of the previous administration. Based on the Appraisal System (Martin & White, 2005), within the framework of Systemic Functional Linguistics (SFL), we specifically look at how this contrast is realized through various linguistic and discourse resources that are used to adopt evaluative stances in relation to both the previous government's actions and his own.

The remainder of the chapter proceeds as follows. In the next section, we discuss different perspectives from which both stance and identity have been studied in relation to language and discourse, and we describe the context of the interviews under scrutiny. Section 3 deals with the study by first outlining the analytical approaches employed, then describing the data collected for the investigation, and finally presenting the analysis of how the president uses language to actively construct a "presidential self" in discursive interaction. Finally, the last section synthesizes the findings and presents some concluding remarks.

2. Background to the study

2.1. Stance

Stancetaking–taking up a position with respect to the form or content of one's utterance–has been studied in different disciplines and from a wide range of perspectives in recent years. In the study of language in relation to the social world, stance has been explored from both a sociolinguistic perspective and a dialogic perspective.

From a sociolinguistic perspective, Jaffe (2009) posits that stancetaking is mainly concerned with positioning:

how speakers and writers are necessarily engaged in positioning themselves vis-à-vis their words and texts (which are embedded in histories of linguistic and textual productions), their interlocutors and audiences (both actual and virtual/projected and imagined) and with respect to that they simultaneously respond to and construct linguistically. (p. 4)

According to Jaffe, in taking a stance, we may observe the interplay between three aspects: personal stance, uptake, and attribution. Firstly, personal stance is concerned with how a linguistic stance may index a given social identity or multiple selves. Secondly, the uptake of stance reflects the dialogic nature of stancetaking (i.e., that stance is emergent in interaction and co-constructed with one's interlocutor). This uptake may take the form of alignment, realignment, or disalignment with prior claims. In doing so, Jaffe argues that stancetaking may contribute implicitly to the naturalization or contestation of certain ideologies (cf. Ibaños, Behle, & Penz, this volume). Finally, the attribution of stance is concerned with the act of projecting a stance onto others (i.e., specifying what the other person's stance is or should be), thus imposing one's own evaluations and attitudes onto other people.

From a dialogic perspective, DuBois (2007) argues that acts of stance are grounded in dialogic and sequential contexts. He makes the claim that the act of taking a stance is not just a linguistic act in the abstract, but also a social act, which is collaboratively and dialogically co-constructed by speakers and their interlocutors in the course of a verbal exchange. Therefore, he proposes a framework for the analysis of stance that takes account of its dialogic nature. For this purpose, he introduces the idea of the stance triangle, in which stance is perceived as a single, unified act made up of three subsidiary acts–evaluation, positioning, and alignment–as well as three sociocognitive relations–objective, subjective, and intersubjective intentionality. According to DuBois, in taking a stance, the subject (i.e., the stancetaker) (a) evaluates an object (the so-called stance object) by orienting to it and characterizing it as having specific quality or value; (b) positions a subject (usually the self) by situating a social actor subjectively with respect to responsibility for the stance and for invoking certain sociocultural values, either affectively or epistemically; and (c) (dis)aligns intersubjectively with the other subjects about a shared stance object (cf. Elder, this volume). All in all, DuBois sums up the act of stancetaking as follows:

Stance is a public act by a social actor, achieved dialogically through overt communicative means of simultaneously evaluating objects, positioning subjects (selves and others) and aligning with other subjects, with respect to any salient dimension of the sociocultural field. (p. 163)

This framework for the stance triangle is illustrated graphically in Figure 6.1 below.

Figure 6.1. The stance triangle

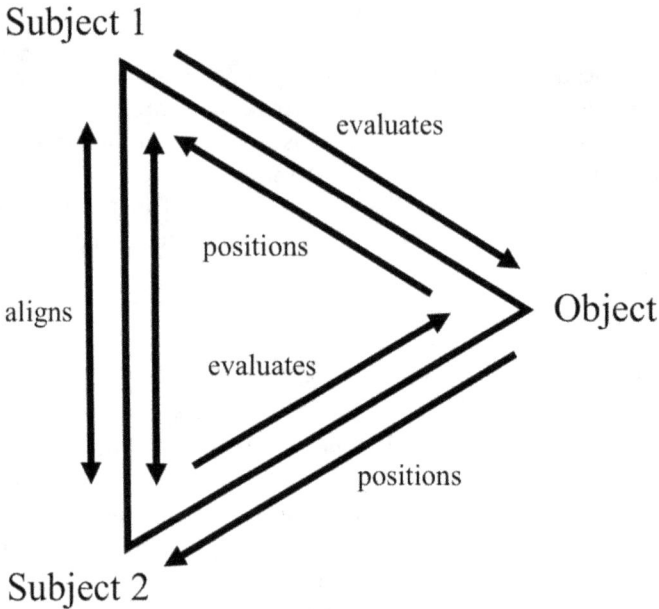

(DuBois, 2007)

The stance triangle is made up of three nodes representing two social actors, subjects 1 and 2, who both separately evaluate a shared object (the third node) and, at the same time, position themselves subjectively to it. In addition, the vertical line on the left represents intersubjective (dis)alignment between the subjects, which may be directed either way, as shown by the two-way arrowheads.

This interactional aspect of the stancetaking process is also taken up by Haddington (2007) in his study of positioning and alignment as stancetaking activities in news interviews. By combining DuBois' theory of stance with Conversation Analysis analytical methods, the author explores the linguistic, sequential, and turn organization in the acts of positioning an alignment. Consequently, in the context of political interviews, he analyzes how, by setting up a position, the interviewers attempt to constrain the possibility for the interviewee to construct a responsive stance. Regarding positioning as an intersubjective activity, Haddington argues that the agenda-shifting actions occasioned by the interviewers' questions trigger aligning activities by means of which "interviewees attempt to find a place to carefully word their stances that not only take into account the evoked and presupposed stances, but also reflect the speaker's own identity, background, aims, and previously stated stances" (p. 311).

Also, in his work on stance and evaluation in political discourse, Spencer-Bennett (2018) focuses on moral talk as a kind of stance act through which people "communicate moral judgements, questions, uncertainties, descriptions and so on" (p. 1). Like most researchers, Spencer-Bennet regards stance and the use of evaluative language to enact stance as an activity that says more about the speaker's values than about their description of the facts of the world. In the same vein, Hunston (2010) suggests that acts of evaluation voice personal opinion so they cannot be objective, and therefore neither true or false, since they are private, subjective acts that are endorsed by speakers.

The evaluative resources employed to enact stance are indexical of the speaker's subjective and intersubjective positioning with respect to what is communicated. This is expressed by Martin and White (2005) in their Appraisal Theory, which is concerned with "the interpersonal in language, with the subjective presence of writers/speakers as they adopt stances towards both the material they present and those with whom they communicate" (p. 1).

In the interviews with President Macri, evaluation is mostly oriented towards the adoption of public stances aimed at doing accountability by praising his own political actions and criticizing the ones carried out by his predecessors in office.

This job of doing accountability contributes to the contestation of different identities that are enacted by the president in the context of the interviews, which provide an opportunity for engaging in impression management.

2.2. Perspectives on identity

With the innumerable social and technological changes in contemporary societies today, the sense of a stable identity has come under threat. As a result, much of the debate on the study of identity revolves around the tensions existing between identity conceptualized as something individuals possess, and identity as negotiated, constructed, or co-constructed in interaction and in relation to broader collective and social groups.

This debate has also been fueled by Bauman's take on identity (Bauman, 2004) as a fluid, fragmented, and unstable social construct that is highly negotiable as a result of a reconfiguration of certain social structures in contemporary society. This reconfiguration gives rise to insecurity in personal relationships, lack of everlasting personal commitment, and increasing social mobility, which, in turn, contributes to the formation of what Bauman (2000) calls "liquid modernity."

The intricate and dynamic nature of identity is also addressed by de Fina, Schiffrin, and Bamberg (2006), and Benwell and Stokoe (2007) who offer a comprehensive review of the different theoretical and methodological perspectives from which identity has been discussed and studied. For these authors, identity is a social product that cannot exist in isolation. Therefore, identity is subject to social influence as it is a social location in which the self is conceived in relation to "its membership of, or identification with a particular group or groups" (Benwell & Stokoe, 2007, p. 24). Moreover, visions of identity as a homogeneous notion have been challenged, giving rise to the conceptualization of identity as a multidimensional discursive practice. Within this view, the authors draw on Goffman (1959) on the performance of identity "premised on a rational, intending self able to manage careful and often idealized, consistent persona or 'front' in order to further his or her personal objectives" (p. 34).

In their work on everyday talk, Tracy and Robles (2013) combine fixed or more stable aspects of the self that are prior to any particular encounter with more dynamic, situated accomplishments enacted through interaction. They distinguish between four types of identities: (a) master identities, relatively unchanging; (b) personal identities, also unchanging but unique to the individual; (c) relational identities, enacted with a particular interlocutor in conversation; and (d) interactional identities, related to role distribution in each specific interactional context.

Parini and Granato (2013) also look at the co-construction of identity in casual conversation by taking language and interaction as the locus of identity work. The analysis of conversations among university students takes into account the dynamic process in the foregrounding and backgrounding of different aspects of self in the unfolding of the discourse.

In this respect, and from a social constructionist perspective, linguistic processes and strategies are seen as central to identity construction. de Fina, Schiffrin and Bamberg (2006) hold that social constructionism has, for a long time now, considered identity as a process that

> 1) takes place in concrete and specific interactional locations, 2) yields constellations of identities instead of individual, monolithic constructs, 3) does not simply emanate from the individual but results from processes of negotiation and entextualization (Bauman and

Briggs 1990) that are eminently social, and 4) 'entails discursive work' (Zimmerman and Wieder 1970). (p. 2)

Other authors working on the relationship between language and identity (Bucholtz & Hall, 2005; Eckert & Rickford, 2001; Englebretson, 2007; Jaffe, 2009, *inter alia*) have centered their attention on the importance of the situated, relational, and ideological aspects of identity construction by looking at stance, position, and style as a way of interconnecting micro, meso, and macro levels of analysis.

In the same vein, and within the political context of Donald Trump's political campaign in running for the American presidency, Sclafani (2018) explores how Trump uses language to project the identity of an authentic, relatable presidential persona. Given the co-constructional nature of identity, Sclafani's work also looks at how the media deal with the intense amount of talk surrounding Donald Trump's use of language.[1]

In our study, President Macri also resorts to language for the projection of the identity of an authentic and relatable head of state who is determined to bring Argentina back into institutional, political and socioeconomic normality.

2.3. The context of the interviews

Political interviews, as representations of broadcast media, have come to occupy a prominent place in the context of political journalism and political communication (Ekström & Patrona, 2011). Because news interviews do not happen in a vacuum, they are better understood as embedded in society and so constitute an organized social institution that stands in relation to other societal organizations, such as journalism and politics. Thus, the political media interview is an instantiation of the link between journalism and politics, and provides a stage on which political discourses can be articulated and where politicians are held accountable for their decisions and actions.

Hoffman (2013) explains that televised political interviews can take different formats where the candidate or interviewee is asked about his or her stances and is forced by the interviewer to defend those positions. Traditional interviews are generally rule-governed and reflect a more orthodox approach to how the communicative situation is staged for an audience that may be present or in absentia or both. However, as Baym (2007) argues, in

---

[1] See Berlin, this volume; Elder, this volume; Ibaños et al., this volume, for discussions specific to Trump's language and language related to Trump in the 2016 US Presidential Campaign.

contemporary, mediatized societies there is an increasing shift to a combination of the traditional interview format and a more conversational, celebrity-type mode of communication. This is also expressed by Hutchby (2011), who argues for a newly evolved type of political interview called the "hybrid political interview" as it exhibits features of both the adversarial political interview and the more everyday, conversational form of talk (cf. Berlin, 2011; forthcoming).

The interviews that we set out to investigate in this paper took place after Mauricio Macri was elected president of Argentina amid the growing discontent of a nation desperate for change. Mauricio Macri, an engineer and the son of an Italian immigrant entrepreneur, became a well-known public figure as the president of Boca Juniors, one of the two most popular football clubs in Argentina. His political career began when he was elected mayor of the city of Buenos Aires in 2003, and his political power was consolidated when he won Argentina's presidential elections on November 22, 2015. The former mayor of Buenos Aires, who ran under the banner of *Cambiemos* (Let's change)–a coalition of mostly centrist non-Peronist parties–won Argentina's second-round, runoff election after defeating Daniel Scioli, Cristina Fernández de Kirchner's favorite candidate and her hand-picked successor. Mauricio Macri was sworn in as president on December 10 in the same year and was expected to reverse the leftist policies of Mrs. Kirchner who had governed the country for two consecutive periods immediately after the end of the presidency of Nestor Kirchner, her husband and political mentor, who governed Argentina from 2003 to 2007, and who died in 2010. Mrs. Kirchner's administration was tainted by corruption scandals and has been accused by the opposition and by a large sector of Argentinian society of favoring a populist and isolationist form of government that pushed the economy towards a crisis.

After taking office, President Macri was interviewed on various prime time TV political talk shows which gave him the opportunity to present himself as a new political leader by doing accountability as a legitimating practice and by performing acts of identity in the discursive construction of his institutional role as a head of state. In all the interviews, framed as question-answer interactional encounters with no live audience, the president was challenged by the journalists to justify how his policies for change and his ideas of the common good were to be articulated in order to address the nation's litany of socioeconomic and political problems. In all cases, the president responded to these challenges by emphasizing the importance for Argentina to have a leader who is visionary, who acts within the constitutional framework, and who espouses republican values. This is a leader who then needs to construct and project the identity of an authentic and empathetic persona, and of a new head of state that distances himself from the bad policies implemented and the unethical values advocated by the previous government.

3. The study

Our study of how President Macri constructs a presidential self in discursive interaction takes into account the institutional and social setting of the interviews, as well as the sociopolitical context in which they occur. We also look at the language resources used by the president to achieve his communicative goals. More specifically, we zero in on the linguistic realizations employed by the president to adopt evaluative stances when doing identity work in his answers to the interviewers' questions.

In line with this view, we adopt the model of language in social context conceived within the field of SFL, able to cope with the complexity of this phenomenon, as Martin and Rose (2008) holds. The authors claim that to examine discourse, two perspectives are required: the relevant levels of language and the three general functions of language in social contexts. The levels, described as the strata of language, are (a) grammar, (b) discourse, and (c) social contexts. These strata operate at different levels of abstraction, going from more abstract (social action) to less abstract (grammar), discourse being in between the two, and the relationship among them is described as one of realization, so that "the social contexts are realized as texts which are realized as sequences of clauses" (p. 4). From this perspective, then, the construction of a text is possible because the grammar of the language offers the necessary sets of resources from which speakers or writers select those alternatives that allow them to express the desired meanings. For SFL linguists, the clause is the unit within which different meanings are expressed in a single grammatical structure which enables them to "show the grammar as a meaning-making resource and to describe grammatical categories by reference to what they mean" (Halliday & Matthiessen, 2004, p. 10) However, they argue that discourses or texts are more than their wordings, as well as social activity is more than the sum of its texts. (Martin & Rose, 2008).

The second perspective required to analyze discourse in an SFL framework is that of the functions that language is used for in social activity, namely (a) the interpersonal metafunction that enacts relationships, (b) the ideational metafunction that represents experience, and (c) the textual metafunction that organizes discourse as meaningful text. These functions are realized simultaneously by different patterns of meaning described as discourse systems (Martin & Rose, 2008). Since a first examination of the interviews revealed that evaluations of different types were the most frequent resources used by the interviewee in the process of stancetaking and in his projection of the identity of a new political leader, our attention will be chiefly centered on the interpersonal metafunction of language, realized by the discourse systems of negotiating attitudes and enacting exchanges, called the Appraisal System.

The Appraisal System, according to Oteíza (2017):

> aims to provide a comprehensive theoretical and descriptive systematization of linguistic resources that can be used to construct the value of social experience, and thereby to achieve a richer understanding of the patterns of interpersonal meaning beyond the manifestation of only emotionality across discourse. (p. 458)

Three dimensions are differentiated within this framework: engagement, attitude, and graduation. Resources of engagement deal with the introduction of only one voice or more than one voice in the production of a text, the choices for the speaker or writer then being monoglossia or heteroglossia, respectively. They also present the discourse producer with alternatives to position himself *vis-à-vis* the contents of an utterance showing different degrees of certainty. Attitude, related to feelings, encloses the evaluative dimensions of affect, judgment, and appreciation. While affect contains resources for the expression of emotional reactions, judgment points to the evaluation of individuals' personal and moral behaviors which can orient to social esteem (how usual, capable, or resolute someone is) or to social sanction (how truthful or ethical someone is). Finally, graduation is concerned with up-scaling and down-scaling attitudinal meanings and has to do with amplification in the two areas of force and focus. Force involves scalar assessments of intensity and amount, and focus refers to the possibility of dealing with categories that can be presented as more or less precise (Martin & Rose, 2008; Martin & White, 2005; Oteíza, 2017).

Among the several developments of the Appraisal System that took place after Martin and White (2005), Oteíza and Pinuer Rodríguez (2012), when dealing with historical processes, elaborate further the domain of appreciation and adds the semantic categories of power, conflict, valuation, and propriety, which allow for a more detailed analysis of events and situations that can be applied to historical, as well as to cultural, phenomena. The category of conflict refers to the way societies can be characterized according to social conflicts "constructed in historical discourses in a very broad manner, such as tension, opposition and contradiction among values, social relations or many others" (Oteíza, 2017, p. 469). Power deals with the activities done by those people or institutions that have the capacity of controlling other less powerful groups, thus exerting an influence on them and limiting their freedom of action. The evaluation of moral or legal issues is done by means of the category of propriety applied to the behavior of historical processes, events, and situations. Finally, valuation refers to the relevance and social value attributed by authors of historical discourses to events, processes, or situations.

3.1. Data and methods

Political discourse and, more specifically, political interviews constitute a fertile arena for politicians to engage in impression management with a view to presenting themselves as trustworthy, capable, and visionary civil servants. This job of doing impression management is carried out not only at the time of campaigning for elections, but also throughout their entire active political lives. Political interviews are ubiquitous in political life, and as they are structured around the frequently challenging questions posed by the interviewers, politicians, as interviewees, cannot evade responding to these challenges. Unlike in most other political discourses, these dynamics in the interaction put considerable pressure on how the politician manages his/her social persona in front of an audience. Therefore, in this case study, we explore the discursive strategies employed by President Macri to present himself as a new political leader in a series of television interviews.

The data are selected from a corpus of six televised interviews with President Macri aired on six primetime TV political shows on Argentinian television between November 2015 and October 2016. The shows are anchored by seven well-known journalists and in six popular programs that were broadcast within the first year of President Macri's administration and that showcased the interviews in different locations: four were carried out in the presidential residence, one of them was conducted in the context of a program that displayed the encounter as a lunch with the president and his wife, and two in different TV studios. The total corpus amounts to two hundred and sixty-six minutes of broadcast material in Spanish, recorded and transcribed for the analysis. The framework of participation consists of four dyadic interactions and two triadic interactions. The dyadic ones include a journalist and the president, whereas one of the triadic ones comprises two journalists and the president, and the other a journalist, the president and his wife.

The style of the interviews varies from fairly formal and conventional to more informal and conversational. This variation in style can be attributed to the relationship between the interviewer and interviewee and especially, the rather informal personal style of the president himself, which creates a relaxed atmosphere that helps frame the interview as a more casual encounter.

In our study, the qualitative analysis of the corpus takes into account the macro, meso, and micro levels of discourse that allow for a better understanding of the meaning-making processes. The macro-level enables us to identify the general characteristics of the social activities under scrutiny, which are situated in a particular post-election sociopolitical context, and through which the president is held accountable to the audience. The meso-level allows us to describe a recurrent rhetorical structure of contrast through which the president evaluates both the previous administration and his own. Finally, the micro-level makes the identification of the semantic and lexicogrammatical resources used in the realization of the rhetorical structure possible. These three levels of analysis offer the background against which the president's stances are analyzed in the process of constructing his presidential persona.

For the purpose of this work, we have translated the material for analysis from Spanish into English. The translations have been rendered as literal as possible so as to keep the functional meaning of language as expressed in the original language. Although the study was carried out on the Spanish version of the material, reference is made to the translated English version of the texts for ease of reading.

3.2. The rhetorical structure of contrast.

A first approach to the analysis of the data allowed us to identify a recurrent rhetorical structure of contrast around which the president organizes his discourse in most of his answers to the journalists' questions. This structure is made up of three steps: in step 1, reference is made to what was done by the previous government; in step 2, reference is made to what has to be done; and in step 3, reference is made to what his government has already done. This structure frequently occurs within the same contribution (i.e., within the same turn), and sometimes it can also be developed in the different turns he takes in the interviews. The steps do not necessarily occur together in one single answer, and even when they do, they may not appear in the same order as described above. Excerpt (1) below exemplifies this rhetorical structure as can be seen in the president's answer.

(1)

ENTREVISTADOR: Macri. Usted ganó las elecciones con un apoyo importante de los votantes y le gente le ha dado una especie de cheque en blanco. Ahora, esta gente, especialmente los que están más preocupados por el dinero dicen: "OK. Está bien lo que el presidente está haciendo, pero quién me cuida el dinero de mi bolsillo con la suba de los precios y los impuestos todos los días," es decir, esta gente que fue la que más sufrió, "Está bien, pero ¿hacia dónde vamos?, ¿pero quién me cuida el dinero?"

MAURICIO MACRI: Lo sé, lo sé, lo sé. Como dije al principio esto me preocupa y todos los días, yo y mi equipo estamos trabajando duro para ver cómo podemos ayudar para que esta reorganización sea menos traumática. Porque tenemos un 700% de inflación acumulada, y encima congelamos las tarifas, entonces tuvimos cortes de energía porque la electricidad era gratis, el sistema de cloacas colapsó porque era gratis, los servicios de agua y gas también colapsaron porque eran gratis. (Step 1) Quiero decir, necesitamos toda esta reorganización para volver a los niveles de energía y agua que teníamos para que nuestros celulares realmente funcionen, para que las empresas puedan crecer, porque sin energía, las empresas no pueden crecer y entonces el empleo no puede crecer y, sin empleo no podemos terminar con la pobreza. Entonces digo, estamos en un punto en el que entendemos qué pasa, (Step 2) y por eso hemos trabajado mucho, Marcelo y Edgardo, para ayudar a los más necesitados. Hoy, alrededor de 5 millones de chicos reciben asignación universal por hijo como resultado de lo que hemos hecho. (Step 3)

Entrevista 1. DV.

INTERVIEWER: Macri, you won the elections with a very important support of the voters and people have given you a bit of a blank cheque, now these people, especially those that are most worried about money, say "ok, that's fine, what the president is doing, but who takes care of the money in my pocket, with prices and taxes increasing every day," I mean, these people are those that were hit the worst, "that's fine but where are we heading for? but who takes care of my own money?"

MAURICIO MACRI: I know, I know, I know, as I said at the beginning, I am worried about this and every day, I and my team are working hard to see how we can help so that this reorganization is less traumatic because we have a 700% accumulated inflation and on top of that we have artificially frozen utility tariffs so we had power outages because electricity was free, the sewage system collapsed because it was free, the water and gas supply services also collapsed because they were free. (Step 1) I mean, we need all this reorganization so that we can get back to the levels of power and water supplies that we used to have, so that our mobile phone actually work, so that business can grow because without energy business cannot grow and so employment cannot grow, and without employment we cannot eradicate poverty. So

I say we are at a stage in which I understand what is happening, (Step 2) and that is why we have also worked hard, Marcelo and Edgardo, to help those that are in need the most. Today about 5 million children get child benefit as a result of what we have done. (Step 3)

Interview 1. DV.

Here, the interviewer poses a question structured around a quotation that brings into the discourse the voice of those who voted for the president and hoped that his administration would change things for the better. This question constitutes a challenge since it demands an explanation from the president as to why this change has not materialized yet, which seems to put his credibility at risk. The president responds to this challenge by making reference to what his government inherited from the previous administration–step 1 of the rhetorical structure. Then, he moves on to focus on the changes that have to be made, and what has to be done–step 2. Finally, he concludes his contribution by stating what he and his government team have already done–step 3. Overall contrast is established by comparing the immediate sociopolitical past with the way the president envisages the future, and with the implementation of his policies and actions so far.

3.3. Negotiating stance in the political interviews

In the interviews scrutinized, the process of stancetaking occurs between the speakers in their roles of interviewer and interviewee. Stances are then adopted and expressed by the president in his answers or reactions to the questions posed by the journalists. These are evaluative reactions through which the president positions himself and, in some cases, (dis)aligns with the interviewers and/or with the audience in absentia (cf. Elder, this volume). This evaluation is manifested in the three steps of the rhetorical structure described above.

For example, in the answer to excerpt (1), negative evaluation occurs in (2) below as the president indirectly criticizes the policies implemented by the previous administration that led to an economic and energy crisis.

(2)

...we have a 700% accumulated inflation and on top of that we have artificially frozen utility tariffs so we had power outages because electricity was free, the sewage system collapsed because it was free, the water and gas supply services also collapsed because they were free.

Interview 1. Step 1.

This evaluation is expressed by means of appraisal resources, both inscribed and invoked. What is evaluatively inscribed here is the critical state the country is in as a result of the wrong policies put into practice by the previous government ("accumulated inflation," "frozen utility tariffs," "power outages," "the sewage system collapsed," "water and gas supply services also collapsed"). By foregrounding these criticisms, the president invokes negative appreciation of the policies implemented by his predecessors in office. At the same, this appreciation alludes to an implicit social sanction–judgment–as it indirectly criticizes the moral actions of those responsible for the wrong decisions taken.

In (3) below, the president shows that he knows what has to be done to find a solution to the problems his government inherited from the Kirchner administration, as expressed in "we need all this reorganization." This reorganization is positively evaluated in terms of the positive results he foresees it will bring about, as shown in "get back to the levels of power and water supplies that we used to have, so that our mobile phones actually work and so that business can grow." Moreover, his argument is supported by highlighting the reasons why his government reorganization plan is the right answer to address these pressing problems.

(3)

I mean, we need all this reorganization so that we can get back to the levels of power and water supplies that we used to have, so that our mobiles phone actually work, so that business can grow because without energy business cannot grow and so employment cannot grow, and without employment we cannot eradicate poverty. So I say we are at a stage in which I understand what is happening.

Interview 1. Step 2.

In (4) below, based on his understating of the problem, the president positively assesses his government actions aimed to relieve the suffering of those who are in need, through the use of the positive appraisal expressions "work hard," "help" and "about 5 million children will get child benefit." These expressions together invoke positive self-judgment as they point to his own moral behavior and that of his government team. These expressions also manifest coherence between his government plans and actions, as well as his concern for those who are deprived of a minimum level of resources to attain a better standard of living.

(4)

We have also worked hard, Marcelo and Edgardo, to help those that are in need the most. Today about 5 million children get child benefit as a result of what we have done.

Interview 1. Step 3.

Evaluation throughout the president's response is reinforced by graduation resources in the stancetaking process. In this way and within this context, up-scaling and down-scaling expressions are employed to convey both positive and negative evaluation. Up-scaling is signalled by means of figures like "700% (negative appraisal)," "5 million" (positive appraisal); intensified lexis like "collapse" (negative appraisal), "eradicate" (positive appraisal); and the use of the adverb "hard" that intensifies the meaning of the verb in the verbal group "work hard" (positive appraisal). On the other hand, down-scaling is manifested through the use of the comparative "less" to convey positive appraisal. Again, these evaluative resources invoke positive moral sanction when his administration is being referred to, and negative moral sanction when the previous administration is alluded to.

In this response, the president positions himself by adopting an epistemic stance in "I know, I know, I know" through which he aligns with the interviewer, and arguably with the citizens whose voice is brought into the talk by the journalist. In the remainder of the answer, affective stances ripple through the text as this is interspersed with instances of inscribed affect revealed by means of the use of the expressions "I am worried" and "I understand"; these expressions denote compassion and understanding and help the president position himself in the discourse.

Apart from positioning self, the president also positions self and others through the employment of the personal pronoun "we" which refers to either himself and all Argentinians as in "We need all this reorganization," or himself and his government team, as in "We have also worked very hard" (cf. Berlin, this volume; Prieto-Mendoza, this volume, for a discussion of the use of personal pronouns in positioning).

In another extract, (5), from a different interview, the president's stances are also framed as evaluative reactions to the interviewer's questions.

(5)

ENTREVISTADOR. Lo que estás proponiendo es un cambio que es más cultural que político.

MAURICIO MACRI: Absolutamente. Es un cambio cultural. (Step 2)

ENTREVISTADOR: Pero es más difícil de lograr.

MAURICIO MACRI: Seguro. Pero es el camino lo que importa. (Step 2)
*Me subí a un avión que estaba a punto de estrellarse, sin instrumentos
porque parte de la locura del gobierno anterior fue destruir todos los
instrumentos, mintiendo sobre la pobreza, pero no hay índices
económicos, los resultados de las pruebas en las escuelas son falsos.*
(Step 1) *Entonces logramos nivelar el avión para evitar estrellarnos,
pero todavía estamos volando sin los instrumentos. Ahora el INDEC está
comenzando a publicar las primeras viras. Vamos a realizar un nuevo
censo, vamos a tomar exámenes confiables.* (Step 3)

INTERVIEWER: What you are proposing is a change that is more
cultural than political

MAURICIO MACRI: Absolutely. This is a cultural change. (Step 2)

INTERVIEWER: But it's more difficult to achieve. (Step 2)

MAURICIO MACRI: Sure, but it is the path taken that matters. I got on
a plane that was on a collision course, without flight instruments,
because part of the craziness (of the previous government) was to
destroy all the instruments, lying about poverty, but there are no
economic indices, national school test results are bogus (Step 1). So,
we managed to level off the plane to avoid a collision but we are still
flying without the proper instruments. Now the National Statistical
Office (INDEC) is beginning to publish the first figures, we are going to
carry out a new census, we are going to carry out reliable school tests.
(Step 3)

Interview 2. PPT.

In fragment (5), the rhetorical structure begins with Step 2 as seen below,
and occurs across two turns in the president's response.

Here, the interviewer's first contribution is expected to elicit a confirmation
from the president. This confirmation is immediately manifested as he says,
"Absolutely. This is a cultural change," through which he first aligns with his
interlocutor and then reinforces this alignment by showing that he knows
what has to be done. The interviewer then makes a brief comment on the
difficulty in producing a cultural change in society, to which the president
reacts by saying "Sure, but it is the path taken that matters," and so once again
he aligns with the journalist, and at the same time acknowledges that this
change is difficult, but it is something that has to be done.

In this context, "cultural change" invokes positive appreciation as this change refers to a profound shakeup in people's attitudes to and views of the sociopolitical organization of the nation, which will help bring about prosperity to all citizens. The phrase "the path taken that matters" also invokes positive appreciation since it refers to the president's own awareness of the right course of action needed to produce such change.

The rhetorical structure in this fragment of the interview continues with the development of step 1 through which the previous government is negatively evaluated, as seen below in (6).

(6)

I got on a plane that was on a collision course, without flight instruments, because part of the craziness (of the previous government) was to destroy all the instruments, lying about poverty, but there are no economic indices, national school test results are bogus.

Interview 2, PPT. Step 1.

By utilizing the metaphor of a plane in distress to refer to the catastrophic situation the country was in when he took office, the president first positions himself using the pronoun "I" by making an invoked negative judgment of his predecessors' inept handling of the state. This is suggested by the use of the noun "craziness" that alludes to an intentional and ill-conceived plan to deceive people by massaging and manipulating economic and education statistics (cf. Ausderan, this volume). In this context, the use of the lexical expressions "lying about poverty," "no economic indices," and "bogus school test results" are employed to convey negative appreciation, as well as to invoke negative moral sanction. Negative appreciation is also manifested employing the metaphoric use of "collision course," "without flight instruments," and "destroy all the instruments."

Finally, in (7), Step 3, the president positively assesses the actions and decisions already taken by his administration.

(7)

So we managed to level off the plane to avoid a collision but we are still flying without the proper instruments. Now the National Statistical Office is beginning to publish the first figures, we are going to carry out a new census, we are going to carry out reliable school tests.

Interview 2, PPT. Step 3.

By resorting again to the plane metaphor, President Macri positions himself and his collaborators by praising his administration's successful strategy to avoid a socioeconomic crisis in "So we managed to level off the plane to avoid a collision." Here "managed to" implies positive appraisal as it conveys success in the president's handling of the situation. But at the same time, he shows caution by acknowledging the fact that the country is not out of the woods yet, as expressed by the negative-evaluative utterance, "but we are still flying without the proper instruments," which means that the country is not completely out of difficulty yet.

Further on in the same interview (Excerpt 8), the interviewer questions the government's decision of not communicating how bad the country's socioeconomic situation was.

(8)

ENTREVISTADOR: Lo que decís es verdad. También es verdad que porque el avión no estrelló y que esto no ayudó a que la gente tomara conciencia de lo difícil que era la situación en la que estábamos, y yo creo que cometieron un error en no explicar exactamente cómo era la situación. ¿Por qué no dijeron en ese momento lo mala que era la situación?

MAURICIO MACRI: Porque necesitábamos un shock de esperanza, felicidad, entusiasmo. Porque fue duro. Pero el 1º de marzo hice hacer un informe que muestra claramente el estado del Estado y te puedo decir que solo puedo dar gracias, gracias a todos los argentinos por su comprensión y su apoyo. He tenido la difícil tarea de tener que dar muy malas noticias y la verdad es que la mayoría de la gente dijo "OK. Si este es el esfuerzo que se requiere de nosotros par hacer un fututo mejor, creemos, todavía tenemos de que, a pesar del fraude y el engaño que se han descubierto en estos diez años que pasaron." Digo este nivel de comprensión de la gente es muy importante, aunque el avión no se estrelló, Jorge, esto muestra una madurez cívica que nunca antes habíamos tenido.

INTERVIEWER: What you are saying is true. It is also true that because the plane hasn't actually crashed and that this hasn't helped people become aware of the difficult situation we were in, and I think you made a mistake by not explaining exactly what the situation was like. Why didn't you say at that moment how bad the situation was?

MAURICIO MACRI: Because we needed a shock of hope, happiness, enthusiasm. Because it was tough. But on March 1, I commissioned a report that clearly shows the state of the State, and I can tell you I can only say thanks, thanks to all Argentinians for their understanding and their support. I have had the difficult task of being the bearer of very bad news and the truth is that most people have said: "OK, if this effort is needed of us to make a better future, we believe, we still have faith in spite of the fraud and deceit that have come to light in these past ten years." I mean this level of understanding from people is very important, although the plane has not crashed, Jorge, this shows a civic maturity we have never had before.

Interview 2, PPT.

President Macri starts his response justifying his actions in "Because we needed a shock...," through the adoption of what Marín-Arrese (2011) and Martín de la Rosa, Domínguez Romero, Pérez Blanco, and Marín-Arrese (this volume) call "effective stance" as he takes a position aimed at influencing reality. In this way, he shows that he knew what all Argentinians, including himself, required after a period of socioeconomic and political turmoil and chaos. This justification is discursively constructed through the verb "need," as well as the nouns "hope," "happiness," and "enthusiasm" which convey positive affect and allude to a process of changing people's feelings and mood based on the conviction that they were downhearted, unhappy and that they lacked enthusiasm. In this justification, he positions himself by indirectly supporting his decision of not explaining how bad the situation of the country was, thus disaligning with the journalist. He presents a counterstance *vis-à-vis* the stance of his interlocutor, who, in his question, remarked: "I think you made a mistake by not explaining exactly what the situation was like."

In the last part of his contribution, the president shows his feelings of satisfaction and gratefulness to the nation in "I can only say thanks, thanks to all Argentinians for their understanding and their support." This utterance as a whole displays positive emotion and invokes positive affect, since it leads to the interpretation that the president is grateful. At the same time, through expressing gratitude to all Argentinians for their understanding and support, he invokes positive social sanction (i.e., Argentinians are understanding and supportive). This is followed by a segment which contains negative and positive evaluations of different stance objects. First, the president conveys negative appreciation of, on the one hand, the duty he had as the head of state in this particular situation by qualifying it as difficult in "difficult task," and, on the other hand, of the news he had to give by qualifying it as very bad in "very bad news," which includes the graduation element "very."

Second, by bringing into his discourse the imaginary voice of the people in the form of a quotation, President Macri positively evaluates the future he is helping to shape as can be inferred from his use of the adjective "better" and the noun "faith" as appreciation resources. He then invokes negative moral sanction of those in charge of the previous administration by resorting to the use of the nouns "fraud" and "deceit," which clearly reveal strong criticism.

Overall, this response contains affective stances in which the interviewee alternates between positioning self by using the pronoun "I" as in "I can tell you...," "I have had the difficult task...," and positioning self and others by using the pronoun "we," which here indexes a category that can be equated with Argentinians, as in "Because we needed a shock of hope," and "a civic maturity we have never had before."

3.4. Constructing the identity of a new political leader

In the unfolding of the interaction, and by means of the stances adopted in the development of the rhetorical structure described above, the president constructs a main type of political identity by foregrounding different aspects of his personal identity that are identified at the micro and meso levels of the discourse, and that recur throughout all the interviews.

At the meso-level of the discourse, developed in one or more question-answer sequences, within which different topics are addressed, these different aspects of identity are manifested through the foregrounding of a moral self, an efficient self, and an affective self. These selves are projected at the micro-level through multiple personal traits. This analysis will make reference to those most salient traits that have a bearing on the construction and projection of the president's identity.

3.4.1. Moral self

The projection of a moral self is instantiated at the micro-level through the stances that the president takes in the development of the rhetorical structure of contrast. A negative stance towards the past administration is adopted in the first step of the structure whereas a positive stance is taken in both the second and the third steps. In the following segments that occurred in the first steps taken from different interviews, the president expresses a strong criticism of what he considers immoral in the policies implemented and the actions taken by his predecessors in office.

(9)

Un gobierno que nos mintió con las estadísticas y la pobreza.

A government that lied to us about statistics and poverty.

Interview 3- GJ

(10)

Un sistema que durante años apretaba a quienes iban en contra de los intereses del gobierno.

A system that for years bullied those who were against the interests of the government.

Interview 3- GJ

(11)

Venimos de una década de un gobierno que predicaba las bondades del estado pero lo destruyó.

For a decade, we had a government that praised the state but destroyed it.

Interview 4- ML

(12)

Se destruyó la credibilidad.

Credibility was destroyed.

Interview 6-JMS.

In the president's discourse, this immoral conduct is conveyed by means of the verbs "lie" (9), "bully" (10), and "destroy" (11 and 12), which signal negative appraisal and, more specifically, moral sanction. In steps 2 and 3 of the rhetorical structure, he adopts a stance that shows that he espouses different moral values, as seen in examples (13)-(16) below.

(13)

Me he comprometido a tener estadísticas confiables.

I have committed myself to proving reliable statistics.

Interview 4. ML

(14)

Tenemos que crear un sistema que diga la verdad.

We have to create a system that tells the truth.

Interview 5-AF

(15)

Tenemos que crear un estado transparente, pero esto es un cambio cultural.

We have to create a transparent state, but this is a cultural change.

Interview 3- GJ

(16)

Yo no gobierno para mí, Yo gobierno para la gente.

I do not govern for myself. I govern for the people.

Interview 6- JMS

Here, the expressions "providing reliable statistics" (13), "to create a system that tells the truth" (14), "to create a transparent state" (15), and "I govern for the people" (16) help the president position himself by using "I" (13 and 16) and "position himself and others" (his team or all Argentinians) by using "we" (14 and 15). In this way, he constructs a moral self by projecting the image of an honest political leader who is committed to his endeavor in office.

3.4.2. Efficient self

The projection of an efficient self is also instantiated at the micro-level of the interviews through the construction of different *personae*. In step 1 of the structure, the president highlights the wrongdoings and mistakes made by the previous government in handling the state, and, on the other hand, in steps 2 and 3, he refers to his own good ideas and achievements.

In the following assertions occurring in step 1, the projection of the image of a competent president hinges on the attribution of incompetence to the past administration.

(17)

La inflación es culpa de un gobierno que administra mal.

Inflation is the result of a bad government administration

Interview 5- AF

(18)

El gobierno pasado para ocultar su incapacidad le echó la culpa a los empresarios.

The past government, in order to hide their incapability, blamed the business sector

Interview 4- ML

In (17), "bad government administration," which clearly refers to the past administration's incompetence, is implicitly contrasted with the good administration of the president's own government and their competence to govern the country. This quality of being competent to govern the country was mentioned throughout his political campaign, and in the interviews where he pledged to lower inflation to normal levels. In (18), by directly attributing incapability to the former government in the phrase "in order to hide their incapability blamed the business sector," the president seems to distance himself from this practice, thus indirectly projecting a capable self.

Given that in steps 2 and 3 reference is made to what the president knows has to be done and to what he has already done, he takes positive stances by positively evaluating his own ideas and actions. These stances contribute to the construction of a self-assured persona. This can be seen in the following fragments.

(19)

Mi trabajo como presidente es generar las condiciones para que haya competencia justa.

My job as a president is to generate the conditions for a fair business competition.

Interview 2. JL

(20)

El camino para la creación de empleo no es inmediato, es una tarea que se hace paso a paso.

The road to the creation of jobs is not instantaneous; it is a step-by-step task.

Interview 1-DV

(21)

La clave para el desarrollo es la confianza.

The key to development is trust.

Interview 6- JMS

(22)

Yo he encarado sincerar los precios de la economía.

I have begun to reconcile prices with the real operating costs.

Interview 5- AF

(23)

Algunos sectores como la energía, la minería y el campo han arrancado.

Some sectors like energy, mining, and farming have already taken off

Interview 4–ML

(24)

Las inversiones estás arribando, el proceso ya comenzó.

Investment is coming to the country; this process is already on its way.

Interview 4–ML

In excerpts (19), (20), and (21), taken from Step 2 of the interview answers, the president uses monoglossic, categorical statements to manifest a kind of reassuring solidity by showing he knows what his job involves, as in "My job as a president is...," "The road to the creation of jobs is...," and "The key to development is..." On the other hand, in (22), (23), and (24), taken from Step 3, the expressions "I have begun to reconcile prices," "Some sectors...have already taken off," and "Investment is coming to the country" are employed to announce that the right policies are already in place to attain his government goals. In the president's view, efficiency in government also includes the capacity and determination of a political leader to work collaboratively with both his government team and society at large. This can be seen in (25), (26), and (27).

(25)

Me reúno periódicamente con los ministros, discutimos temas, trabajamos como equipo.

I have regular meetings with the ministers; we discuss issues, we work as a team.

Interview 3–GJ

(26)

Vamos a solucionar esto, nosotros, los argentinos, trabajando juntos en equipo.

We will sort this out, we Argentinians, working together as a team.

Interview 1- DV

(27)

Nosotros, los argentinos, todos tenemos que entender que somos miembros del mismo equipo, la Argentina.

We, Argentinians, all have to understand that we are members of the same team, Argentina.

Interview 2- JL

In these fragments from his responses, President Macri projects himself as not being a one-man band or self-centered political leader as expressed in the use of "work as a team" (25), "working together as a team" (26), and "we are members of same team" (27) where the word "team," as in many other fragments throughout the interviews, fulfills a prominent discursive role in casting the identity of an efficient self.

3.4.3. Affective self

The third aspect of the president's personal identity that is enacted in the interactions with the journalists is concerned with the manifestation of emotions and affect that lead to the projection of the image of a caring, empathetic, and understanding political leader, that is a leader who is not out of touch with people's sufferings. This is shown in fragments (28), (29), and (30).

(28)

Yo sé lo que pasa en nuestro país, y lo lamento.

I know what is going on in our country, and I feel sorry for it.

Interview 6–JMS

(29)

Yo tengo que ocuparme de ayudar a aquellos que son débiles.

I have to take the job of helping those who are weak.

Interview 5- AF

(30)

Empezás a pensar qué es lo importante y que es lo no importante, y lo importante es el afecto, el afecto en general, el poder dar.

You begin to think what is important and what is not, and the important thing is affect, in general, to be able to help.

Interview 3- GJ

These fragments occur in steps 2 and 3, and sometimes outside the rhetorical structure. Here the affect-laden expressions "feel sorry" (28), "help those who are weak" (29), and "affect" (30) are used to construct and adopt a positive affective stance. In (28), the president first refers to his awareness of the problems affecting the country by adopting an epistemic stance signalled by "I know what is going on in our country." This is immediately followed by the formulation of affective stance as expressed in "I feel sorry for it," which reveals his personal concern and feelings about the difficult times Argentina is going through. By expressing his commitment to easing the suffering of those in need in (29), President Macri positions himself by taking personal responsibility in "I have to take the job of...," and at the same time exhibits sensitivity in "help those who are weak."

Finally, in (30) and on a more personal note, the president voices the great value he attributes to affect in human relationships in "the important thing is affect, affect in general, being able to help." Here, he speaks as an ordinary man rather than a head of state. This affective self, together with a moral self and an efficient self, helps activate multiple identities that are constructed around the values of sensitivity, rectitude, and aptitude, brought into the discourse as the president's most salient personal traits. At a macro-level, then, these multiple identities build up an image of a president who is radically different from his predecessors and who helps legitimize a new way of doing politics and governing the country.

4. Conclusion

In this chapter, we have analyzed the stances taken by the president in the construction of a rhetorical structure of contrast, as seen in his responses to interviewers' elicitations. In this relational process of stancetaking, the contrastive rhetoric of "us"–his own government–versus "them"–the previous government–is exploited as a central mechanism for the co-construction of his political identity.

In the contemporary Argentinian political context, this political identity depicts a refreshing political leader who distances himself from past leaders, and who proposes a necessary and sensible change to govern the country. This macro identity is propped up by different aspects of his personal and social identities that are negotiated at a micro-level in the interviews. Consequently, these projected identities are the ones that he seems to believe will help him gain support from the audience in his endeavor to construct a prosperous nation.

The employment of a rhetorical structure of contrast at the meso level and the utilization of the semantic system of appraisal at the micro-level constitute the main discourse strategies the president resorts to in the act of performing the identity of a new political leader. This identity is made up of different aspects of self that are foregrounded in the interactions, and that can be collapsed into a moral self, an efficient self, and an affective self.

These fluid and emergent types of identities are occasioned, indexed, and made relevant in the course of the ongoing interaction within the communicative situation of the interviews, and against the background of the local political and socioeconomic context. These interviews then, serve as critical sites for identity work and contestation in contemporary society where politicians need to confront the ways in which situated identity performances shift swiftly and straddle diverse interactional contexts in order to cope with the rapidly reconfiguring nature of interpersonal relationships and social conducts.

References

Andone, C. (2013). Strategic maneuvering in a political interview: The case of responding to an accusation of inconsistency. In A. Fetzer (Ed.) *The pragmatics of political discourse* (pp. 103-124). Amsterdam/Philadelphia: John Benjamins.

Ausderan, J. (2020). Oh, that's just crazy talk: How leaders use language to create perceptions of irrationality. In L. N. Berlin (Ed.), *Positioning and stance in political discourse: The individual, the party, and the party line,* (pp. 55-69). Wilmington, DE: Vernon Press.

Baym, G. (2007). Crafting new communicative models in the televisual sphere: Political interviews on *The Daily Show. The Communication Review, 10* (2), 93-115.

Bamberg, M., de Fina, A., & Shiffrin, D. (Eds.) (2007). *Selves and identity in narrative and discourse.* Amsterdam/ Philadelphia: John Benjamins.

Bauman, R., & Briggs, C. (1990). Poetics and performance as critical perspectives on language and social life. *Annual Review of Anthropology, 19,* 59-88.

Bauman, Z. (2000). *Liquid modernity.* Cambridge: Polity Press.

Bauman, Z. (2004). *Identity: Conversations with Benedetto Vecchi.* Cambridge: Polity Press.

Benwell, B., & Stokoe, E. (2007). *Discourse and identity.* Edinburgh: Edinburgh University Press.

Berlin, L. N. (2011). *El Modelo Multinivel de Contexto: un marco para explorar la manipulación del lenguaje y la manera en que lo mediático y lo político se fusionan en un discurso híbrido. Discurso & Sociedad, 5* (1), 9-40.

Berlin, L. N. (2020). The positioning of post-truth politics: Claims and evidence in the 2016 US presidential campaigns. In L. N. Berlin (Ed.), *Positioning and stance in political discourse: The individual, the party, and the party line,* (pp. 1-30). Wilmington, DE: Vernon Press.

Berlin, L. N. (forthcoming). Positioning the voices of conflict: Language manipulation in the Diálogos de Paz. In I. Chiluwa (Ed.), *Discourses of conflict and conflict resolution.* Amsterdam/Philadelphia: John Benjamins.

Bucholtz, M., & Hall, K. (2005). Identity and interaction: A sociocultural linguistic approach. *Discourse Studies, 7* (4-5), 585-614.

de Fina, A., Schriffin, D., & Bamberg, M. (Eds.) (2006). *Discourse and identity.* Cambridge: Cambridge University Press.

DuBois, J. (2007). The stance triangle. In R. Englebretson (Ed.), *Stancetaking in discourse: Subjectivity, evaluation, interaction* (pp. 139-182). Amsterdam/Philadelphia: John Benjamins.

Eckert, P., & Rickford, J. R. (Eds.) (2001). *Style and sociolinguistic variation.* New York: Cambridge University Press.

Ekstöm, M., & Patrona, M. (Eds.) (2011). *Talking politics in broadcast media: Cross-cultural perspectives on political interviewing, journalism and accountability.* Amsterdam/Philadelphia: John Benjamins.

Elder, C. (2020). Trump vs. Clinton: Implicatures as public stance acts. In L. N. Berlin (Ed.), *Positioning and stance in political discourse: The individual, the party, and the party line,* (pp. 71-91). Wilmington, DE: Vernon Press.

Englebretson, R. (2007). *Stancetaking in discourse: Subjectivity, evaluation, interaction.* Amsterdam: John Benjamins.

Goffman, E. (1959). The presentation of self in everyday talk. New York: Doubleday.

Haddington, P. (2007). Positioning and alignment as activities of stancetaking in news interviews. In R. Englebretson (Ed.), *Stancetaking in discourse: Subjectivity, evaluation, interaction* (pp. 283-318). Amsterdam/Philadelphia: John Benjamins.

Halliday, M. A. K., & Matthiessen, C. (2004). *An introduction to functional grammar* (3rd ed.). London: Hodder Education.

Hoffman, L. (2013). Political interviews: Examining perceived media bias and effects across TV entertainment formats. *International Journal of Communication, 7,* 471-488.

Hunston, S. (2010). *Corpus approaches to evaluation.* London: Routledge.

Hutchby, I. (2011). Non-neutrality and argument in the hybrid political interview. *Discourse Studies, 13* (3), 349-366.

Jaffe, A. (2009). *Stance: Sociolinguistic perspectives.* Oxford: Oxford University Press.

Lakoff, R. T. (2005) The politics of nice. *Journal of Politeness Research, 1,* 173-191.

Marín-Arrese, J. I. (2011). Effective vs. epistemic stance and subjectivity in political discourse: Legitimising strategies and mystification of responsibility. In C. Hart (Ed.), *Critical discourse studies in context and cognition* (pp. 193-223). Amsterdam/Philadelphia: John Benjamins.

Martin, J. R., & Rose, D. (2008). *Working with discourse: Meaning beyond the clause.* London and New York: Continuum.

Martin, J. R., & White, P. R. R. (2005). *The language of evaluation: Appraisal in English.* New York: Palgrave Macmillan.

Martín de la Rosa, V., Domínguez Romero, E., Pérez Blanco, M., & Marín-Arrese, J. I. (2020). Epistemic and effective stance in political discourse: The European refugee crisis. In L. N. Berlin (Ed.), *Positioning and stance in political discourse: The individual, the party, and the party line,* (pp. 141-156). Wilmington, DE: Vernon Press.

Oteiza, T. (2017). The appraisal framework and discourse analysis. In T. Bartlett & G. O'Grady (Eds.), *The Routledge Handbook of Systemic Functional Linguistics* (pp. 457–472). London/New York: Routledge.

Oteíza, T., & Pinuer Rodríguez, C. (2012). Prosodia valorativa: Construcción de eventos y procesos en el discurso de la historia. *Discurso & Sociedad, 6* (2), 418-446.

Parini, A., & Granato, L. (2013). Negotiating identities in casual argumentative conversation. *Łodz Papers in Pragmatics, 9* (2), 134-141.

Prieto-Mendoza, M. A. (2020). Positioning in the peace process: Stance during the Colombian Peace Dialogues. In L. N. Berlin (Ed.), *Positioning and stance in political discourse: The individual, the party, and the party line,* (pp. 31-53). Wilmington, DE: Vernon Press.

Sclafani, J. (2018). *Talking Donald Trump: A sociolinguistic study of style, metadiscourse, and political identity.* London: Routledge.

Spencer-Bennet, J. (2018). *Moral talk: Stance and evaluation in political discourse.* London: Routledge.

Tracy, K., & Robles, J. (2013). *Everyday talk. Building and reflecting identities.* London: The Guildford Press.

Zimmerman, D. H., & Wieder, D. L. (1970). An ethnomethodology and the problem of order: Comment on Denzin. In J. D. Douglas (Ed.), *Understanding everyday life: Towards a reconstruction of sociological knowledge* (pp. 285-295). Chicago: Aldine Publishing.

Chapter 7

Epistemic and Effective Stance in Political Discourse: The European Refugee Crisis[1]

Victoria Martín de la Rosa*, Elena Domínguez Romero*, María Pérez Blanco**, and Juana I. Marín-Arrese*
*Universidad Complutense de Madrid, Spain
**Universidad de León, Spain

Abstract

This chapter addresses a key issue in United Kingdom political discourse: the expression of epistemic or effective stance by politicians with respect to the issue of immigration, migration, and the refugee crisis in Europe, which is often presented as a potential "threat" for the UK. The multifaceted nature of stance has been associated with notions, such as affect, attitude, evaluation, and engagement in discourse (Biber & Finegan, 1989; DuBois, 2007; Englebretson, 2007; Hunston & Thompson, 2000; Marín-Arrese, 2013; Martin & White, 2005; Ochs & Schieffelin, 1989; *inter alia*). In this chapter, the framework for the analysis draws on a model of stancetaking in discourse which posits two macro-categories of stance: the *epistemic*, or the expression of speaker/writer's beliefs, knowledge, or evidence that support or justify their claims in making an assertion, and the *effective*, or the expression of speaker/writer's attitude with regard to potential actions and plans for action (Marín-Arrese, 2009; 2011a; 2011b; 2015a; 2015b). We here focus on the distribution and use of epistemic and effective stance resources by UK politicians, representing the ideological spectrum from the far-right and center-right to the center-left, and the extent to which the similarities or differences in discourse strategies may reflect varying political positionings

---

[1] This research has received support from the project *Stance and Subjectivity in Discourse: Towards an Integrated Framework for the Analysis of Epistemicity, Effectivity, Evaluation and Inter/Subjectivity from a Critical Discourse Perspective* (STANCEDISC), Ref. PGC2018-095798-B-I00, funded by the *Ministerio de Ciencia, Innovación y Universidades* [Spanish Ministry of Science, Innovation and Universities].

with regard to the issue of immigration in the UK (Clayman, 2017). The chapter presents a case study on the use of epistemic and effective stance markers in the discourse on immigration in the political speeches and the electoral manifestos for 2015 and 2017 of a number of political parties, namely the UK Independence Party (UKIP), the Conservative Party, and the Labour Party, as representatives of far-right, center-right, and center-left ideologies.

1. Introduction

This chapter explores the expression of speaker/writer stance in the discourse of politicians in the UK with respect to the issue of immigration, migration, and the refugee crisis in Europe. We focus on the use of epistemic and effective stance strategies in the discourse of a number of political parties in the UK, representing the ideological spectrum from the far-right and center-right to the center-left. The chapter addresses the following issues: (a) the similarities or differences in the distribution and usage of effective and epistemic stance resources by politicians along the left to right ideological spectrum; and (b) the extent to which they reflect differences in discourse strategies linked to political positioning with regard to the issue of immigration on the basis of the presumed ideologies of the parties.

It is hypothesized that striving for epistemic and effective control in political discourse will be more visible in those contexts where more is felt to be at stake and where there is a greater perceived need for legitimizing plans of action and ideologies, in this case, the "sense of nationhood" (Joseph, 2006), and the presumed potential "threat" posed by immigrants for the UK. Variation may also be found due to possible differences in discourse practices and styles of persuasion of individual speakers/writers.

The chapter presents a case study on the use of epistemic and effective stance markers in the discourse on immigration in the political speeches of politicians and electoral manifestos of a number of political parties, namely the UKIP, the Conservative Party, and the Labour Party, as representatives of right, center-right, and center-left ideologies.

Section 2 presents the theoretical framework for the analysis of the data; section 3 describes the methodology. In section 4, we present the results and discussion, and the final section is devoted to the conclusions.

2. Literature Review and Theoretical Framework

There is a tradition in discourse studies, as Martin and White (2005) note, in which "all utterances are seen as in some way stanced or attitudinal" (p. 92). The multifaceted nature of stance has been associated with concepts, such as affect, attitude, evaluation, and engagement in interaction (Biber & Finegan, 1989; DuBois, 2007; Englebretson 2007; Hunston & Thompson, 2000; Marín-Arrese, 2013; Ochs & Schieffelin, 1989; *inter alia*) (cf. Elder, this volume). Within the various perspectives on stance, Englebretson (2007) observes that there are five key conceptual principles in common:

> (1) stancetaking occurs on three (often overlapping) levels–stance is physical action, stance is personal attitude/belief/evaluation, and stance is social morality; (2) stance is public, and is perceivable, interpretable, and available for inspection by others ... ; (3) stance is interactional in nature–it is collaboratively constructed among participants, and with respect to other stances ... ; (4) stance is indexical (cf. Haviland 1989; Silverstein 1976), evoking aspects of the broader sociocultural framework or physical contexts in which it occurs; (5) stance is consequential–i.e., taking a stand leads to real consequences for the persons or institutions involved. (p. 6)

We here focus on the notion of stance as a form of social action, involving the expression of the speaker/writer's personal beliefs concerning the status of the event and their commitment with respect to the communicated proposition. An additional crucial notion of stance with regard to the event is that of speaker/writer's positioning with respect to determining or influencing the course of events themselves. This paper draws on a model for the analysis of stancetaking in discourse, which posits two macro-categories of stance: the epistemic and the effective (Marín-Arrese, 2009; 2011a). These categories draw on Langacker's (2009; 2013) distinction between the epistemic and the effective level in the grammar of the language, and the way in which these categories reflect the systematic opposition between striving for control of conceptions of reality and striving for control of relations at the level of reality. Marín-Arrese (2013) defines these categories of stance in the following terms:

> Epistemic stance (henceforth EP) pertains to the positioning of the speaker/writer with respect to knowledge concerning the event and their commitment to the validity of the information. These are stance acts assessing the reality of the event designated or the likelihood of its realization, and/or specifying the sources whereby the speaker/writer feels entitled to make an assertion, which may involve an estimation of their evidentiary reliability.

> Effective stance (henceforth EF) pertains to the positioning of the speaker/writer with respect to the realization of events, to the ways in which the speaker/writer carries out a stance act aimed at determining or influencing the course of reality itself. (p. 414)

Epistemic stance strategies involve the use of epistemic modals, evidentials, and expressions of cognitive attitude and factivity to convey speaker/writer's beliefs, knowledge, or evidence that support the truth of a proposition or the validity of its content (Boye, 2012; Capelli, 2007; Kiparsky & Kiparsky, 1970; Marín-Arrese, 2009; 2011a). Effective stance strategies involve the "speaker/writer's expression of norms, obligations and compelling, or enabling circumstances, and of his/her inclination, decision or intention to carry out an event" (Marín-Arrese, 2013, p. 411).

The use of stance resources in the discourse may serve to index ideological positioning and political identity of speakers/writers (cf. Parini & Granato, this volume). In this respect, it is relevant to quote Bucholtz and Hall (2005), who define identity as "the social positioning of self and other" (p. 585), and argue that identity is a sociocultural phenomenon, which is intersubjectively produced and constituted discursively. They point out that among other linguistic expressions, identities may be linguistically indexed through specific stances.

Epistemic and effective stance strategies may be exploited by politicians as legitimization strategies for purposes of persuasion or manipulation, with the specific aim of persuading hearers/readers of the benefits of particular policies and action plans. Epistemic legitimization strategies (Hart, 2011; Marín-Arrese, 2011b) function indirectly by providing epistemic justification and epistemic support for the proposition (Boye, 2012), thus reflecting speaker/writer's commitment with respect to knowledge, which may be crucial in persuading the audience about the benefits of particular actions and plans for action. However, the expression of speaker's commitment or lack of commitment, as Berlin (2008) observes, may also be due to the speaker's choice in seeking to strategically boost, or alternatively attenuate, the force of an assertion in order to "align more closely with or distance himself or herself from the assertion through the degree of commitment expressed" (p. 375), independently of his/her belief in the content of the assertion. Effective stance strategies function directly by claiming the desirability, normativity, or requirement of those actions and plans for action (Chilton, 2004; Marín-Arrese, 2011a). As van Dijk (2006) and Maillat and Oswald (2009) have pointed out, making others believe and do things is one of the main components of manipulative language use (cf. Berlin, this volume).

3. Methodology and data

3.1. The corpus

This paper examines a number of political speeches and electoral manifestos of three political parties, representative of right, center-right, and center-left ideologies in the United Kingdom, namely, the UKIP, the Conservative Party, and the Labour Party. The texts examined were produced between 2015 and 2017 and have been mainly downloaded from the official parties' websites.

The corpus includes two genres of political discourse: written manifestos and oral speeches. The oral speeches analyzed were given by the respective party leaders and other party politicians as follows:

Labour Party: Jeremy Corbin (15 speeches) + 9 individual speeches by politicians such as John McDonnell or Sarah Champio. (Source: http://press.labour.org.uk/)

Conservative Party: Theresa May (15 speeches) + 10 individual speeches by other politicians: Ruth Davidson or David Davis, among others. (Source: http://press.conservatives.com/)

UK Independence Party: Nigel Farage (9 speeches), Henry Bolton (4 speeches), David Kurten (2 speeches), Jim Carver (2 speeches), Paul Nuttal (2 speeches), Steven Woolfe (2 speeches) + 5 individual speeches given by Paul Griffith, Diane James, Peter Lundgren, Steven Crowther, and David Coburn. (Source: http://www.ukip.org/news & different newspapers)

The total size of the corpus is of approximately 175,000 words comprising both the transcripts of oral speeches (164,335 words) and the written manifestos (9,890 words). Table 7.1 shows the total size of the corpus of political texts, together with the distribution per political party and genre.

Table 7.1. Corpus of political texts: Sources, genres, and number of words

CORPUS	ORAL: Speeches	WRITTEN: Manifestos	TOTAL
LABOUR	56,029	2,337	58,366
CONSERVATIVE	55,228	2,177	57,405
UKIP	53,078	5,376	58,454
TOTAL	164,335	9,890	**174,225**

3.2. Research objectives and procedure

This chapter presents a case study on the expression of stance and the indexing of political positioning in the discourse of politicians in the UK with respect to the issue of migration and the refugee crisis in Europe. It has been hypothesized that striving for epistemic and effective control in political discourse will be more salient in contexts where there is a greater perceived need for legitimizing plans of action and ideologies, in this case, regarding the presumed potential "threat" posed by immigrants to the UK. In order to test this hypothesis, the present research aims to:

(a) characterize the presence and patterning of the expression of effective and epistemic stance in the discourse of the three political parties by identifying and quantifying the various linguistic resources used.

(b) explore the similarities or differences in the use of these resources by three political parties, representing the ideological spectrum from the far-right and center-right to the center-left, in order to reveal the rhetorical potential of these resources and the exploitation of their persuasive effects by the speakers.

Focusing on these research objectives, the texts were examined and tagged manually to identify the effective and epistemic markers retrieved from the corpus. The examples found were then classified and quantified according to the categories given for the expression of effective and epistemic stance.

4. Results and discussion

This paper has explored the types of legitimizing strategies deployed in the discourse of three political parties along the left to right ideological spectrum and how they are exploited by speakers/writers for the rhetorical goal of persuasion.

4.1. Qualitative analysis

4.1.1. Epistemic stance

Epistemic stance resources include modal and evidential markers, as well as expressions of factivity and cognitive attitude, whereby the speaker/writer expresses degrees of certainty regarding the reality status of the event, assessment of the evidentiary validity of the proposition designating the event, and/or beliefs regarding the realization of the events. Within epistemic stance, the following subcategories may be identified (cf. Marín-Arrese, 2011a; 2015b) to classify the lexico-grammatical categories we found in our corpus:

(a) Epistemic modality (EM): Epistemic modals; adverbs, predicative adjectives.

(1) "...we have to make people understand this *may* <EP, EM> be the last opportunity ever get to become a normal country once again." (UKIP)

(2) "*Perhaps* <EP, EM> if the Chancellor had spent less time thinking up stale jokes, and a little more time thinking through the consequences of what he was proposing, he wouldn't have ended up in this mess." (Labour)

(3) "And in the last few days, we have seen just how tough these talks *are likely* <EP, EM> to be." (Conservative)

(b) Indirect Inferential Evidentiality (IIE): Predicates of perceptual-based or conceptual-based inferences; adverbs and predicative adjectives.

(4) "And in the last few days, *we have seen* <EP, IIE> just how tough these talks are likely to be." (Conservative)

(5) "Two thirds of Labour MPs represent constituencies that voted to leave; one third represent constituencies that voted to remain. This is *obviously* <EP, IIE> a difficult decision." (Labour)

(6) "But *it is clear* <EP, IIE> that this Conservative Government has its focus elsewhere." (Labour)

(c) Cognitive Attitude (CGA): Personal predicates of mental state and belief.

(7) "I'm taking nothing for granted but *I think* <EP, CGA> we're going to do well in the European elections. My ambition, my conviction is that we can come first and cause an earthquake." (UKIP)

(8) "*We believe* <EP, CGA> that government action now is vital to reduce the impact on smaller businesses, and move towards making the local business taxation system fairer and closer to the real economy." (Labour)

(d) Factivity (FTV): Personal and impersonal predicates expressing factive meaning.

(9) "As **we all know** (EP, FTV) seventeen point four million people voted to leave the European Union and this party has a moral obligation given our role in that process to ensure..." (UKIP)

(10) "**The fact** <EP, FTV> that the wealthy can seemingly dodge their taxes at will has further undermined public confidence in the tax system." (Labour)

4.1.2 Effective stance

Effective stance resources include root modals, semi-modals, modal adjectives and nouns, expressions of directivity, and personal predicates expressing intentionality, normativity, or potentiality. Drawing on Marín-Arrese (2011a; 2015a), we have grouped the lexico-grammatical categories found in our corpus under the following subcategories of effective stance:

(a) **Deontic modality (DM)**: Deontic modals, semi-modals, and modal adjectives and nouns of possibility and necessity.

(11) "Britain is one that we can and should look forward to while this is a new era for our country **we must** (EF, DM) be honest and say that this is a new era for all of us in this room a new era for UK the Brexit" (UKIP)

(12) "The UK, **we need** <EF, DM> to ensure we've got an equally strong mandate and an equally strong negotiating position." (Conservative)

(13) "This is the exact opposite of how the tax system **is supposed** <EF, DM> to function, and clearly out of line with best practice elsewhere." (Labour)

(14) "It was with reluctance that I decided the country needs this election but it is with strong conviction that I say **it is necessary** <EF, DM> to secure the strong and stable leadership the country needs to see us through Brexit and beyond." (Conservative)

(b) **Directivity (DIR)**: Hortatives and other expressions with a conventional directive force, and personal predicates with lexical directive meaning.

(15) "**Let us** <EF, DIR> tomorrow vote for an election, **let us** <EF, DIR> put forward our plans for Brexit and our alternative programmes for government and then let the people decide." (Conservative)

(16) "The Lords have passed Labour's amendment and *we urge* <EF, DIR> the government to immediately bring forward a guarantee to protect the rights of all EU nationals resident here. (Labour)

(c) **Intentionality (INT)**: Modals of volition and personal predicates expressing inclination, intention, or commitment.

(17) "I can give you this commitment *I will* (EF, INT) be behind you *I will* (EF, INT) make sure that you get the support you need..." (UKIP)

(18) "*We want* <EF, INT> our large corporations to work for the public good–not against it." (Labour)

(d) **Normativity (NRM)**: Personal and impersonal predicates expressing desirability or normativity.

(19) "To ensure the future of our country as well as UKIP success, *it is essential* <EF, NRM> that the membership fully support the next leader of our party, whoever wins the contest, and work as hard as we have in the past." (UKIP)

(20) "Because as I say, this is an election in which every single vote counts. So *it is important* <EF, NRM> that we get out there." (Conservative)

(21) "*It's about time to* <EF, NRM> ensure that we eliminate intrinsic, structural barriers that prevent people from reaching their full economic potential." (Labour)

(e) **Potentiality (POT)**: Modals and other expressions of possibility.

(22) "It means, in theory, *we can* <EF, POT> deliver the same high-quality public services across the whole country." (Labour)

(23) "*It is an opportunity* <EF, POT> to change this country for the better for the future, *it's an opportunity* <EF, POT> to ensure that this really is a country that works for everyone and not just the privileged few." (Conservative)

The following section outlines the methodology applied in our case study and the description of the corpus of political speeches and party manifestos.

4.2. Quantitative analysis

4.2.1. Categories of epistemic stance in political discourse

Epistemic legitimization strategies signal authorial commitment to the validity of the information and thus provide epistemic support for the proposed policies and action plans. Table 7.2 shows the categories of epistemic stance found in the discourse of the three political parties. The results are given in raw numbers and normalized frequencies in a ratio per thousand words.

Table 7.2. Categories of epistemic stance in political discourse

EPISTEMIC STANCE	Labour (58,366 words)		Conservative (57,405 words)		UKIP (58,454 words)		Total (174,225 words)	
	N	R	*N*	R	*N*	R	*N*	R
EM	22	0.377	47	0.819	60	1.026	129	0.740
IIE	5	0.085	4	0.069	4	0.068	13	0.075
CGA	26	0.445	31	0.540	69	1.180	126	0.723
FTV	46	0.788	56	0.975	9	0.154	111	0.637
TOTAL	99	1.696	138	2.403	142	2.429	379	2.175

Labour discourse differs from the other two political groups in that it is characterized by a considerably lower use of epistemic stance markers (R=1.696), with the only exception of the expression of factive meanings (R=0.788). The lowest ratio of epistemic modality markers would reflect a higher degree of commitment to truth. In this respect, concerning epistemicity and truth, Bybee, Perkins, and Pagliuca (1994) observe that "markers of epistemic modality indicate something about less than a total commitment by the speaker to the truth of the proposition" (p. 179). In other words, Labour discourse seems to be the most committed, as it shows a low frequency of epistemic modality markers (R=0.377).

Conservative discourse also shows a clear preference for presenting information as facts, as uncontested knowledge (R=0.975). Nevertheless, it also evinces a considerable reliance on epistemic markers (R=0.819), which brings it close to UKIP (R=1.026) with the highest use of this type of marker. It may be said that Conservative discourse is characterized by a balance between factive predicates (R=0.975) and epistemic markers (R=0.819).

UKIP discourse presents distinctive features which set it aside from the political discourse of the other two parties. It uses the highest ratio of epistemic stance strategies (R=2.429), closely followed by Conservative discourse (R=2.403). In particular, UKIP shows the highest ratio for epistemic markers (R=1.026). The far-right political discourse of UKIP is also characterized by the highest ratio of cognitive attitude predicates (R=1.18). This makes UKIP discourse less committed to truth and more subjective, in contrast with the discourse of Conservative and Labour Parties that favor the expression of factive meanings.

Looking altogether at the data for epistemic stance, the political discourse of the Conservative Party seems to be halfway between the discourse of Labour, both Labour and Conservative favoring factive markers (FTV), and the discourse of UKIP, with which it shares its high reliance on epistemic support of the information (EM).

The discourse of the three political groups shows very low reliance on evidential justification for the information. Indirect inferential markers stand at the lower end of the cline across the three political parties.

4.2.2. Categories of effective stance in political discourse

Effective stance resources are used by the writers/speakers to exert control on the realization of an event by claiming its necessity or desirability. This second type of legitimization strategy is deontic and functions at the level of reality. The raw numbers and normalized frequencies for the categories of effective stance found in the discourse of the three political parties are shown in Table 7.3 below.

Table 7.3. Categories of effective stance in political discourse

EFFECTIVE STANCE	Labour (58,366 words)		Conservative (57,405 words)		UKIP (58,454 words)		Total (174,225 words)	
	N	*R*	*N*	*R*	*N*	*R*	*N*	*R*
DM	191	3.272	280	4.877	286	4.893	757	4.345
DIR	24	0.411	50	0.871	11	0.188	85	0.488
INT	223	3.821	329	5.731	134	2.292	686	3.937
NRM	15	0.257	33	0.574	2	0.034	50	0.287
POT	29	0.497	64	1.115	32	0.547	125	0.717
TOTAL	482	8.258	756	13.169	465	7.955	1,703	9.775

Conservative discourse shows the highest ratio for effective stance (R=13.169), well over that of Labour (R=8.258) and UKIP (R=7.955). Its rhetoric mainly relies on expressions of intention and commitment (R=5.731), closely followed by the use of deontic markers (R=4.877).

Similar to Conservative, Labour discourse is also oriented towards the expression of intentions (R=3.821) and the necessity of the realization of events (R=3.272). However, a more moderate discourse seems to be preferred, as ratios for the abovementioned effective stance markers are considerably lower.

UKIP discourse prioritizes deontic markers (R=4.893), followed far behind by modals of volition and personal predicates expressing intentions and commitment (R=2.292). It is interesting to see that UKIP discourse is very close to the Conservative Party discourse regarding the use of deontic markers. However, UKIP's general ratio for effective stance strategies is considerably lower due to its markedly lower reliance on modals of volition and commitment.

The lowest values are found for normativity markers (NRM) across all three parties, which tend to present a shared responsibility.

4.2.3 Epistemic vs. effective stance markers

Table 7.4 illustrates the global use of epistemic and effective stance resources in the discourse of the three political parties, representing the left to right ideological spectrum in the UK. Both types of legitimizing strategies are aimed at persuading hearers/readers of the benefit of adopting the proposed plans of action.

Table 7.4. Epistemic vs. effective stance markers in political discourse

STANCE	Labour (58,366 words)		Conservative (57,405 words)		UKIP (58,454 words)		Total (174,225 words)	
	N	R	*N*	R	*N*	R	*N*	R
EPISTEMIC STANCE	99	1.696	138	2.403	142	2.429	379	2.175
EFFECTIVE STANCE	482	8.258	756	13.169	465	7.955	1,703	9.774
TOTAL	581	9.954	894	15.574	607	10.384	2,082	11.95

The discourse of the three political parties is characterized by a considerably lower use of epistemic stance markers, with UKIP showing the highest ratio. Normalized frequencies range from lower to higher as follows: Labour Party (R=1.696), Conservative Party (R=2.403), UKIP Party (R=2.429).

The figures for effective stance are considerably higher for the three parties, with Conservatives showing the highest ratio (R=13.169). Conservative discourse is well ahead of the Labour Party (R=8.258) and UKIP (R=7.955). Effective stance markers underscore the position of the parties in terms of intentions/promises/commitments, and of the necessity of the realization of events.

Summing up the similarities and differences in the expression of epistemic stance in the political discourse of the three parties, it can be observed that both the UKIP Party and the Conservative Party have the highest ratios of epistemic stance. However, the Conservative Party stands out for its more recurrent use of effective strategies (R=13.169 versus R=8.285 for Labour and R=7.955 for UKIP) involving the legitimation of the realization of actions, which are exploited for the rhetorical goal of persuasion.

Differences are also observed in the type of resources used by the three political parties for the expression of both epistemic and effective stance. In the case of effective stance, Conservative and Labour prioritize intentionality (R=5.731, Conservative; R=3.821, Labour). The two parties make a similar use of effective stance markers, with differences mainly relying on frequency of use. Alternatively, UKIP discourse favors deonticity (R=4.893), whereas modals of volition and personal predicates expressing intention fall far behind (R=2.292).

In the case of epistemic stance, data place Conservative discourse (R=2.403) in an intermediate position between Labour (R=1.696) and UKIP (R=2.429), close to Labour in the category factive markers (FTV) and close to UKIP in the use of epistemic modals (EM).

5. Conclusions

This chapter has explored the expression of speaker/writer stance in the political discourse of a number of political parties in the UK, with respect to the issue of migration and the refugee crisis. In this corpus-based study, we have analyzed and characterized the epistemic and effective stance resources used by three parties along the left to right ideological spectrum to legitimize their ideologies and plans of action. Epistemic and effective stance markers are used by speakers/writers as devices for exerting control over conceptions of reality or the course of reality itself (Langacker, 2009; Marín-Arrese, 2009; 2011b), acting as rhetorical mechanisms aimed at persuading the audience.

The study has confirmed that stance markers are particularly noticeable in the discourse of political parties either in power or in the opposition, especially when, as in the case of the European refugee crisis, there is a crucial controversial issue requiring action to be first legitimized and then taken. As shown in this chapter, the three political parties, namely the UKIP, the Conservative Party, and the Labour Party exploit epistemic and stance strategies to persuade hearers/readers of the benefits of their policies. However, significant differences have been found in the distribution of the various stance resources, resulting in the prioritization of different discourse strategies. The particular discourse practices and styles of the three parties would reflect their different ideologies, and might also be influenced by their role in the current political scenario.

In terms of epistemic stance, Conservative and Labour discourse strategies are more based on facts, whereas UKIP discourse is more tentative and less committed to truth (Bybee et al., 1994). However, it is interesting to point out that Conservative discourse is also characterized by a relatively high reliance on epistemic markers, indicating less than full commitment to the validity of the information. In other words, it has been observed that, in terms of epistemic stance, the discourse strategy of the Conservative Party is based on striking a balance between the expression of factive meanings, presenting information as uncontested knowledge, and a lack of complete commitment to the validity status of the communicated propositions.

At the effective level, with respect to the realization of events, UKIP plays a leading role in demanding the UK Parliament take action. UKIP political discourse is characterized by an extensive use of expressions of deonticity, whereas it shows a much lower frequency of markers of volition and personal predicates expressing intention or commitment. In other words, the UKIP Party calls for action in the UK Parliament, while showing less internal commitment to action.

Conservative and Labour Party discourses, on the other hand, focus more on promises and explicit expressions of intention to take future actions. Effective stance strategies, especially intention markers, are particularly salient in the discourse of the Conservative Party. They present themselves as knowledgeable of what is in the best interests of citizens, which creates a rhetoric of power that legitimizes their proposed plans of action by claiming to "be right in a moral sense" (Chilton, 2004, p. 117). Meanwhile, the Labour Party, in the opposition role, shows a comparatively lower ratio of deontic and intention markers, distancing itself from the discourse of the Conservative Party.

In summary, it can be said that the discourse of the Conservative Party is the one more fully loaded in terms of the number of epistemic and effective markers used in legitimizing their proposed courses of action. On the other hand, the discourses of the Labour and the UKIP Parties do not rely so heavily on the use of those resources. However, it is also true that the three political parties give more weight to the use of effective than epistemic stance markers, where the necessity or desirability of an action is clearly expressed.

For further research, it would also be worth looking into how the discourse of each party progresses in relation to the issue of migration and the refugee crisis so as to see whether their use of epistemic and effective markers remain the same or new ways to legitimize their proposed courses of action arise.

References

Berlin, L. N. (2008). I think, therefore ...": Commitment in political testimony. *Journal of Language and Social Psychology, 27* (4), 372-383.

Berlin, L. N. (2020). The positioning of post-truth politics: Claims and evidence in the 2016 US presidential campaigns. In L. N. Berlin (Ed.), *Positioning and stance in political discourse: The individual, the party, and the party line*, (pp. 1-30). Wilmington, DE: Vernon Press.

Biber, D., & Finegan, E. (1989). Styles of stance in English: Lexical and grammatical marking of evidentiality and affect. *Text, 1*, 93-124.

Boye, K. (2012). *Epistemic meaning: A crosslinguistic and functional-cognitive study*. Berlin: Mouton de Gruyter.

Bucholtz, M., & Hall, K. (2005). Identity and interaction: A sociocultural linguistic approach. *Discourse Studies, 7* (4-5), 585-614.

Bybee, J., Perkins, R., & Pagliuca, W. (1994). *The evolution of grammar: Tense, aspect, and modality in the languages of the world*. Chicago: University of Chicago Press.

Capelli, G. (2007). *"I reckon I know how Leonardo da Vinci must have felt..."*: *Epistemicity, evidentiality and English verbs of cognitive attitude*. Pari: Pari Publishing.

Chilton, P. (2004). *Analysing political discourse*. London: Routledge.

Clayman, S. E. (2017). The micropolitics of legitimacy: Political positioning and journalistic scrutiny at the boundary of the mainstream. *Social Psychology Quarterly, 80* (1), 41–64.

DuBois, J. W. (2007). The stance triangle. In R. Englebretson (Ed.), *Stancetaking in discourse: Subjectivity, evaluation, interaction* (pp.139-182). Amsterdam/Philadelphia: John Benjamins.

Elder, C. (2020). Trump vs. Clinton: Implicatures as public stance acts. In L. N. Berlin (Ed.), *Positioning and stance in political discourse: The individual, the party, and the party line*, (pp. 71-91). Wilmington, DE: Vernon Press.

Englebretson, R. (2007). Introduction. In R. Englebretson (Ed.), *Stancetaking in discourse: Subjectivity, evaluation, interaction* (pp. 1-26). Amsterdam/Philadelphia: John Benjamins.

Hart, C. (2011). Legitimising assertions and the logico-rhetorical module: Evidence and epistemic vigilance in media discourse on immigration. *Discourse Studies, 13* (6), 751-769.

Hunston, S., & Thompson, G. (Eds.) (2000). *Evaluation in text: Authorial stance and the construction of discourse*. Oxford: Oxford University Press.

Joseph, J. E. (2006). *Language and politics.* Edinburgh: Edinburgh University Press.

Kiparsky, P., & Kiparsky, C. (1970). Fact. In M. Bierwisch & Karl E. Heidolph (Eds.) *Progress in linguistics* (pp. 143-73). The Hague: Mouton.

Langacker, R. W. (2009). *Investigations in cognitive grammar.* Berlin: Mouton de Gruyter.

Langacker, R. W. (2013). Modals: Striving for control. In J. I. Marín-Arrese, M. Carretero, J. Arús, & J. van der Auwera (Eds.) *English modality: Core, periphery and evidentiality* (pp. 3-55). Berlin: Mouton de Gruyter.

Maillat, D., & Oswald, S. (2009). Defining manipulative discourse: The pragmatics of cognitive Illusions. *International Review of Pragmatics, 1* (2), 348-370.

Marín-Arrese, J. I. (2011a). Effective vs. epistemic stance and subjectivity in political discourse: Legitimising strategies and mystification of responsibility. In C. Hart (Ed.), *Critical discourse studies in context and cognition* (pp. 193-223). Amsterdam: John Benjamins.

Marín-Arrese, J. I. (2011b). Epistemic legitimising strategies, commitment and accountability in discourse. *Discourse Studies, 13* (6), 789-797.

Marín Arrese, J. I. (2013). Stancetaking and inter/subjectivity in the Iraq inquiry: Blair vs. Brown. In J. I. Marín-Arrese, M. Carretero, J. Arús, and J. van der Auwera (Eds.), *English modality: Core, periphery and evidentiality* (pp. 411-445). Berlin: Mouton de Gruyter.

Marín-Arrese, J. I. (2015a). Effective control in political discourse: A cross-linguistic study of text-related variation. Paper presented at the *48th Annual Meeting of the Societas Linguistica Europaea,* 2-5 September 2015, Leiden University Centre for Linguistics (LUCL), Leiden.

Marín-Arrese, J. I. (2015b). Epistemic legitimisation and inter/subjectivity in the discourse of parliamentary and public inquiries: A contrastive case study. *Critical Discourse Studies, 12* (3), 261-278.

Martin, J. R., & White, P. R. R. (2005). *The language of evaluation. Appraisal in English.* Basingstoke/New York: Palgrave Macmillan.

Ochs, E., & Schieffelin, B. (1989). Language has a heart: The pragmatics of affect. *Text, 9* (1), 7-25.

Parini, A., & Granato, L. (2020). Stance in casting the identity of a new political leader: Interviews with the President of Argentina. In L. N. Berlin (Ed.), *Positioning and stance in political discourse: The individual, the party, and the party line,* (pp. 109-139). Wilmington, DE: Vernon Press.

van Dijk, T. (2006). Discourse and manipulation. *Discourse and Society, 17* (3), 359-383.

Index

www.ingramcontent.com/pod-product-compliance
Lightning Source LLC
Chambersburg PA
CBHW050517280326
41932CB00014B/2360